THE
BOOK
OF
CONTRASTS

or, the
Thirty-second
Chapter
of
Proverbs

The Book of Contrasts

or, the Thirty-second Chapter of Proverbs

DAVE STRICKLAND

ATHENA PRESS

LONDON

ISBN 978 1 84748 557 1

First published 2009 by
ATHENA PRESS
Queen's House, 2 Holly Road
Twickenham TW1 4EG
United Kingdom

Printed for Athena Press

DEDICATED TO HELEN KELLER
who came to see and hear in this world as clearly as she sees and hears in the world where she is now.

Prologue

To experience a settled stomach and avoid discomfort, digest the sayings in *THE BOOK OF CONTRASTS* slowly. Are you rushing around too fast in your life and finding it hard to slow up and reflect? If that is you, you're missing an awful lot of important things – and for what? Take a rest – you're a human being, not a human doing.

I want to make an impassioned plea. When you read this volume, try to cast out of your mind the questions 'Who wrote it? How old is he? What does he look like? Does he have a day job? What is his star sign?' It really isn't important. On the other hand, people are irremediably curious, so after thinking about it I decided to reverse my original intention and allow my identity to be associated with the book. After all, any writer with a heart should value his readership, observe their reactions and heed their observations. Much better if you have an idea of the person behind the prose. For the curious, then, I am male, I was born in 1948, a true-to-type Gemini (sun sign, not star sign), and I work for a living. Well, that's enough about me: why an impassioned plea? The reasons are to be found within the pages of the book itself, and you are urged to ponder sayings 148, 296, 444, 565 and 1169 for the reasons in question. Yes, I'm sure you would rather gaze at an amethyst or an emerald rather than a pebble. It was Thomas à Kempis who centuries ago instructed his readers, 'Don't pay regard to who said a certain thing; pay regard to what was said.'

It is not as though those of the sayings in this volume which are new (which are probably half of them) are really from me. They are the diamonds while my own brain is just a pebble. I have been shown a wonderful apple tree and invited to pick choice apples from it to share with the world. Without being at all religious about it, there is a God and there is a world of Spirit. The only contribution I want to think I have personally made to

THE BOOK OF CONTRASTS is that many years ago I decided to talk to God. I said to Him that if He were ever to offer me a gift, the one I would want most would be to be like Solomon in the Bible and be a wise person. But I'd have to draw the line at cutting babies in half. It wasn't really a good idea to ask the Supreme Being of the universe for next week's lottery numbers in advance so I could end up with a posh house and a flash sports car... or be a handsome hunk with a muscular body so I could impress all the women in my life. These things never last anyway, and I've yet to see a dead man of eighty in a coffin who is still the possessor of a fabulous physique (and hair), or one covered in banknotes which he's going to take with him to spend in Heaven.

How *THE BOOK OF CONTRASTS* has come to be

That request to God was a long time ago when I was a callow youth. Life went on as normal as the next man's, year upon year. At some point I started paying attention to the wise sayings of the world, those one- or two-liners which you come across in innumerable books and magazines. I pondered over the wise people in the world who said a lot in the fewest possible number of words, and this was in contrast to the much more common verbal diarrhoea I encountered. As I mused on this comparison, some time in the year 2007, I began to experience something unusual. Equally succinct messages and insights, concerning all aspects of everyday life, began to enter and fill my mind: complete life principles in single sentences, and it was not long before these statements became a torrent.

There was nothing dramatic about this experience, no audible voices, flashing lights or trances, just sayings quietly inserted into my mind. So I questioned God. He seemed to be saying to me, 'Well, son, you asked for wisdom. Here's a boat load of it. Don't lose them: write them all down and you won't forget them.' The difficulty was, I'd be right in the middle of doing all the normal things poets do, like driving a bus or carrying building materials (paid work I've had), and I'd find myself scrabbling round for bits of paper to scribble down the thoughts which spontaneously entered my head. I would then put them into proper English and add them to what was steadily becoming a sizeable anthology.

I saw that there was a sort of common theme to these sayings: the contrasting of ideas which were in opposition to each other. I was beginning to appreciate two things: that equilibrium in life is achieved by *the balancing of opposing states*; and that seeing an idea's opposite throws that idea into relief and shows it up for what it really is. I discerned these same perceptual mechanisms in many of the existing sayings I had pondered over, so I decided to single out and sometimes reword these ones too, mixing them in with my own. No doubt many readers of *THE BOOK OF CON-TRASTS* will recognise various of these other sayings, gems which have sprung from the lips or pens of wise people, contemplative souls who have hailed from many places and times. I would like to think the reader would share the perception I have, that *THE BOOK OF CONTRASTS* is a reflective commentary on the human condition.

Publish and be damned – or publish and others be saved?

I wasn't thinking about publishing these sayings. The idea might have seemed presumptuous, and presumption is a sin. But the idea was gradually forming that other people might benefit from contemplating the terse utterances I was collecting together. Vanity is another sin (one of the Deadly Seven, no less), and I wanted that character defect to be denied any claim to life. Readers are to receive, not a book from a wise author, but a wise book from an author. The *true* authors of *THE BOOK OF CONTRASTS* reside firmly in the world of spirit, from God downwards. I am but the guardian of these sayings.

As there is largely no order to the sayings, this volume lends itself to random sampling anywhere within its pages. There is a small Roman Catholic book on angelic sayings I came across which is similar: it suggests you think of a different number each day and then look up the saying against that number. This is what you can do with *THE BOOK OF CONTRASTS*, dip into it as you would sample the contents of a box of chocolates. As I mused over the question of publishing, I placed another question before God and the spirit guardians in my life: 'Do you want me to do this? If you do, you'll have to make it clear.' At this time the total number of sayings I'd collected had reached about 500, and I figured I might struggle to achieve many more. The idea of the total reaching the number filling this volume seemed simply unrealistic, and I wasn't playing a numbers game anyway. The fact that sayings continued to enter my head was one reason I learned that I should pursue publication. And the sayings have not ceased to come to me, which necessitates a cut-off point for this book.

Having committed *THE BOOK OF CONTRASTS* to publication, it is necessary to point up a few things. Around half of the sayings are from the pens and lips of other people, and around half are my own. But this is a very rough estimate because I have not made a count of them. For the sayings of other people, I have taken the liberty of editing them, rewording them, or adding to them. I'm sure their authors wouldn't have minded in the least because I've taken extreme care to preserve the spirit of what they said. Many of them wrote in foreign languages anyway. I have seen fit to make explicit reference to the authors of a certain few sayings where so doing seems to enhance the message itself, or where I might inflict dishonour on them by the omitting their names. My personal favourite saying of all time is the one I feel deeply should be the one at the very conclusion of this book. It is well known, a quatrain from *The Rubáiyát of Omar Khayyám*. My father used to repeat it slowly to us with grave dramatic effect, as was his style, and it made a deep impression on me. Come to think of it, this was the very first wise saying I ever consciously thought about and reflected upon. It was one of the very few things I can recite from memory. Over time I lovingly did my own polishing of the English translation of that quatrain as an alternative to that of Fitzgerald in the *Oxford Dictionary of Quotations*, but it is his which is preserved in this book.

Reflections

If *THE BOOK OF CONTRASTS* causes only a few people to become (more) aware of what life is really about, it will have been well worth the publishing effort. I am cognisant of an emphasis expressed in the pages of this book; that is, the desire to depict material life in a spiritual context, and not the world of spirit as a take-it-or-leave-it adjunct or disposable appendage to material life. Our lives are but a vapour. You might not think this now, while you are young and vibrant and enjoying life, but wait until you're on your deathbed and thinking over your past years… and reflecting on what is to come! You can't escape it. Yes, but fret not: live your life as you should and you will have nothing to fear. You don't have to be perfect, only to desire it and try your best. In any case, how could God ever demonstrate His patience and forbearance unless you got up His nostrils?

Notice I've said nothing about religion. God isn't a religion and Jesus is not religious. And one of the surest ways of getting sidetracked in your life is to take it up. This is a secondary emphasis in the book, one where I have allowed myself to express criticism. And it is directed to all the religious phoneys of the world, many of whom you will recognise wherever you live. By expressing observations about religious phoneys through the medium of these sayings, it is hoped people can be guided who search for spiritual realities, but who are susceptible to being drawn in and sucked down false alleyways. It is personal experience which serves as the springboard for my dissection of religious beliefs.

It is our approach to religion which elicits the most salutary of all life's contrasts. I illustrate this: people perceive the Ten Commandments as the means adopted by the Almighty of kicking us into line, regulations which preclude any ducking of our moral responsibilities. If only. But there happen to be more ancient ordinances. One is a code of forty-two statements of moral responsibility; another is comprised of twenty-two holy questions.[*]

Did you spot it? The contrast, of course. The Ten Commandments are a set of DOs and DON'Ts; the *Twenty-Two* are QUESTIONS. No risk is attendant on imposing instructions

---

[*] These sets of ancient ordinances sometimes crop up in obscure works of esoteric literature. Unfortunately, the sources I accessed to discover them are no longer available for me to identify and cite for the reader.

upon your creatures. In contrast, it is risky indeed to defer to the possibility that your creatures may opt to defy your wishes. But whom would you rather have in life: someone who does what is right out of obligation or fear, or someone who chooses the right out of a voluntary inner choice?

With the Ten Commandments, you don't have to think, just do; with the *Twenty-Two* (and the *Forty-Two* statements) you have to make decisions. The Old Testament commands, 'Thou shalt not steal'; the *Twenty-Two* ask 'Have you caused pain or loss to another man or creature?' With the Commandments, you can claim innocence for theft, yet find innumerable ways to cheat and hurt your fellow man. They are the epitome of religion, and religious phoneys exploit them for all they are worth to kick sinful ass (as the Americans would say), or to do our thinking for us. In contrast, codes such as the *Forty-Two* or the *Twenty-Two* are the epitome of spirituality. Responsibility for your life is on your own shoulders, not mine or the publisher's; it is the epitome of ill decision-making to devote this duty over to others.

Thus are you invited to absorb the sayings of *THE BOOK OF CONTRASTS*. It is an antidote to all false approaches to life. Dip into its pages as you would raid a biscuit barrel. And, as the Irish comedian Dave Allen said, 'May your God go with you…'

Dave Strickland
Doncaster, England
dave@strickland669.orangehome.co.uk

THE BOOK OF CONTRASTS
or, the Thirty-second Chapter of Proverbs

The photographs included in this volume are from the author's collection of scenes of the places where he grew up as a child, and have hardly changed over the years. They all depict the county of Lincolnshire in the East Midlands of England. Most were taken on the author's travels as a delivery courier; he always had his camera to hand. To the author, tarmac roads in a countryside setting are a metaphor for the path one journeys on through life.

1. Happiness is not having what you want, but wanting what you have.

2. Fashion is made only to become unfashionable.

3. Beauty is the first gift nature gives to a woman, and the first it takes away.

4. There is no odour so bad as that which arises from goodness tainted.

5. Misfortunes are like knives: they either cut us or serve us, according to whether we grasp them by the blade or by the handle.

6. Personality is the need to feel a sense of being acceptable and loveable without having to qualify for that acceptance.

7. To him who is in fear everything rustles.

8. Hasten not to do good to: no. 1. The ungrateful – they neither value your goodness nor contemplate the virtue.

9.   Say nothing good of yourself and you will be distrusted; say nothing bad of yourself and you will be taken at your word.

10.   It is well to read something of everything and everything of something.

11.   A book is like a mirror: if an ass looks into it, can an angel look out?

12.   If you tear yourself away from the safe comfort of certainties for the sake of truth, then you will be rewarded by the certainty of truth.

13.   The tallest trees are those which are most exposed to the winds, and ambitious men to the blasts of fortune.

14.   Happiness is not a state to arrive at; it is a means of travelling.

15.   Hasten not to do good to: no. 2. The idle – your goodness serves only to encourage them in their idleness.

16.   They will say you are on the wrong road if it is your own – or if it is not theirs.

17.   The most dangerous people are the ignorant.

18.   You influence the manner in which people treat you by how you treat yourself.

19.   Be cautious in believing the compliments people give you or the criticisms they level at others.

20.   Knowledge humbles the great, astonishes the common, and puffs up the small.

21.   Love is not blind; but because it sees more it is willing to see less.

22.   A person in a Christian society who embraces paganism should take care he is not trading his wings for his feet.

23.   The resolved mind has no cares.

24. Speak when you are angry and you will make the best speech you will ever regret.

25. Hasten not to do good to: no. 3. The indolent – your goodness serves only to dissuade them from exercising what is necessary for them to help themselves.

26. When it is dark enough you can see the stars.

27. My father didn't tell me how to live. He lived and I watched him.

28. Courage is the art of being the only one who knows you're scared to death.

29. Once the game is over, the king and the pawn go back into the same box.

30. Hasten not to do good to: no. 4. Those who say 'Aha!' to your offer of goodness and make selfish use of it.

31. He who waits to do a great deal of good at once will never do anything.

32. To lead people, walk behind them.

33. I felt sorry for myself because I had no shoes – until I met a man who had no feet.

34. If you have a dream, give it a chance to happen.

35. He enjoys much who is thankful for little.

36. Many come to bring their clothes to church rather than themselves.

37. Hasten not to do good to: no. 5. Those who refuse to help themselves but instead look to others to bail them out.

38. As a remedy against all ills, poverty, weariness, sickness and melancholy, there is but one cure-all: a liking for work.

39. You must first see before you can believe. Even those who believe but do not see, they see with faith, because faith has its own eyes.

40.	Do not do what you would undo if you were in danger of being caught.

41.	All wish to possess knowledge, but few are willing to pay the price.

42.	A romance is where each person plays a part the other really likes.

43.	In romantic love you desire the other person; in real love you desire the other person's good.

44.	Why is it called free love when those who indulge in it become slaves to their passion?

45.	You don't always win your battles, but it's good to know you fought them.

46.	The injustice done to an individual is sometimes of service to the wider public.

47.	Real friends are those who, when you've let them down, don't regard you as having done a permanent job.

48.	One who has lost confidence has nothing more he can lose.

49.	What we all look for are blessings not in disguise.

50.	The joys or the troubles we expect are not so bright, or so dark, as we expect them to be.

51.	The surest way to pierce a woman's heart is to kneel down and aim upwards.

52.	Hasten not to do good to: no. 6. The opportunist – he despises your goodness but misses no chance to jump up and avail himself of it.

53.	Learn to pause – or nothing worthwhile will catch up to you.

54.	Conscience is the inner voice which warns us someone may be looking.

55.   Were we as eloquent as angels we still would please people much more by listening rather than talking.

56.   The plainer the dress, the greater lustre doth beauty possess.

57.   If you want to go on hating someone, better that you avoid learning about him; you may discover things in him you can love.

58.   No temptation can gravitate to a man unless there is that in his heart which is capable of responding to it.

59.   All women are flirts; with shy women their shyness restrains them.

60.   Many a Christian is one who feels repentance on Sunday for what he did on Saturday and is going to do on Monday.

61.   Beauties in vain their pretty eyes may roll:
Charms strike the sight, but merit wins the soul.

62.   It may be beyond your capabilities to change the world, but you can change *your* world.

63.   You can gain the respect of others only if you first respect yourself.

64.   Is it right or wrong to do it? To ascertain which, imagine doing it alone in a room and your God suddenly opening the door and walking in.

65.   Hasten not to do good to: no. 7. Those who take for granted that this is the way things should be – you give; they take.

66.   The ship of life is loaded on one side with Compassion and on the other side with Justice. To capsize the ship, merely remove one of these virtues.

67.   It is better to aid the deserving though you benefit the unworthy, than it is to deprive the deserving in order to withhold good from the unworthy.

68.   A vulgar term: the difference between the word 'breasts' and the word 'tits' is that the latter are flaunted in public: a vulgar term for a vulgar habit.

69.   A true conqueror is he who gains mastery over his own soul.

70.   A wise man knows he walks among both the wise and the foolish; a fool is too dull to know he walks among the wise as well as his own kind.

71.   There are those who give the appearance of strength and endurance, but drop them on the stone floor of life and they shatter. Bend like a reed in the wind.

72.   A witness to endurance. Many times I passed a tree whose trunk was long ago charred and gutted by lightning into a gnarled, hollow stump. Year by year it continued to bear a healthy amount of fresh foliage.

73.   Beware how you pray to God: you might just receive what you ask Him for.

74.   Hasten not to do good to: no. 8. Those who regard you as soft and weak instead of kind and good.

75.   It is better to be hated than ignored. When you are ignored you don't count for anything.

76.   A wise man does not often act out of the impulse of conviction but out of calm judgment that his act is right.

77.   If you visit your father, do you promptly open your mouth and gabble on without interruption, showing a lack of interest in his reception of you? Please, O Christian, show me another way to pray.

78.   A reasonable and fair man countenances the sincere views of others with whom he disagrees. Even better is he who listens in patience to such views and at their conclusion pauses, only then commencing to give a response.

79.   It is better to do good to one person than to punish seven enemies.

80.   Listen to or watch, not what a man says or does, but what he omits to say or do.

81.   In desiring the love of the opposite sex, first love and seek friendship, forgetting that this person is of the opposite sex.

82.   Mercy which pardons evil is darkness disguised as light. The merciful pardon the man, but not his evil.

83.   Men lose money in the vicissitudes of misfortune. Gamblers work out how to do it.

84.   Hasten not to do good to: no. 9. Those who squander the help you give them by wasting and ruining what you yourself have always maintained carefully.

85.   Prayers of equal importance to God: that of a world leader who implores Him to send peace to mankind, and that of a child who cries to Him because someone broke his toy.

86. Aim to reach 100% success and you may attain 80%; aim for your 80% and you may attain only 60%.

87. A man's strength is measured not by what he achieves but by what he endures.

88. A fool compares himself to a bigger fool and thinks himself wise.

89. Many who encounter shortcomings in marriage embrace them as an excuse for infidelity. True love embraces fidelity as the means to remedy shortcomings.

90. A guilty man is loud and ostentatious in his display of innocence. The man standing in quietude before his accusers deserves a true hearing from them.

91. When two people vociferously accuse each other before a hearer, Wisdom whispers to him that the truth lies comfortably in the middle.

92. Many people are animal lovers because they decline the harder task of loving their own species.

93. The most apt picture of a man's life is the hourglass. The sands of time drain inexorably away, but the glass can be turned over.

94. It is said that the mind of a man condemned to die in two weeks is concentrated wonderfully. Alas, his death does not bring his state of mind to an end; it continues to be fixed in that state by the record of his life presented before him.

95. If your words are no better than your silence, better your silence.

96. Hasten not to do good to: no. 10. The irresponsible – their troubles are of their own making.

97. Do not hasten to open your mouth to a stranger. The less he knows about you, the more he may respect what he can only guess about you.

98. Guard the previous saying when you woo your beloved, and you will win her through her curiosity and fascination with the unknown you.

99. He who calls himself a master is unworthy of the title.

100. Do not fear death; but you may have need to fear its aftermath.

101. Suicide: a permanent solution to a temporary problem.

102. If a man remains silent, is that because he has nothing to say?

103. You don't take your empty soul to church where God awaits you to fill it; you take your God to an empty building for worship and fill that.

104. Hasten not to do good to: no. 11. Those who come to you with sob stories and pluck woeful tunes on the strings of your heart.

105. I pointed at the moon and a fool looked at my finger.

106. Which will you choose? A gold nugget covered with mud; or a sparkling gilt ring? Choose the first and you will be in the minority. You doubt that? Then ponder how men in fine clothes and possessed of a display of worldly goods are accepted, and the poor in rags are despised or ignored.

107. If someone is more crippled than you are crippled, that is reason enough to attend to his needs.

108. Don't blame the gun when the victim has been shot dead. The gun was minding its own business lying in the drawer until someone picked it up.

109. An innocent young woman who draws attention to her sexuality unawares is in danger of joining company with her experienced streetwise counterparts. Male eyes react to the outward form, not the inner soul.

110. A man can never be a law unto himself: all through his life he trades one set of masters for another.

111. The value of a man's opinion is measured by what it cost him to arrive at it.

112. Surprised to encounter ingratitude from your boss after you have shown yourself willing to go the extra mile for him, moreover in perfect devotion and honesty? Not such a surprise: many in number are the bosses who would not rise to be like you if the roles were reversed.

113. If a man has a passion to destroy, let him destroy the power which his passions exercise over him.

114. It is not a good thing to hate; hatred without a legitimate object to direct it towards consumes the hater.

115. If a man orders you to do something, do not jump up in a fever of haste to obey or oblige. Pause and only then be prompt and resolved.

116. When you give reply to a man who has spoken, do not hasten to an immediate retort or observation. Pause, reflect, and only then speak, and do so in measured tones.

117. When you greet a friend or stranger with a hearty welcome, do not switch off your smile or avert from him your gaze the instant he turns his head away. A bystander who sees you will note your insincerity. You cannot switch off genuine greetings in your heart as you can your face.

118. Always seek to give a reason for obliging someone to do, or to desist from doing, something. If a child, he especially will appreciate you for this. Few are the occasions when reasons cannot be conveniently given.

119. The God of the Old Testament is said to be vindictive and cruel, eschewed by those who embrace the loving God of the New. What, then, will you do with this loving God who sees and permits the vindictiveness and cruelty of *men*?

120. Many are the roads which lead up the mountain towards God at the summit: all true roads reach and merge thereat.

121. Heaven for a sinner who has not earned it quickly becomes Hell.

122. Hasten not to do good to: no. 12. The con artist – he invents sore needs and devises how he can profit from your sympathy.

123. A subject to be faced: as there is a fine line between one's genitalia and one's organ of elimination, so is there a fine line between selfless love and selfish lust.

124. The secret of winning hearts and minds is in avoiding bruising the egos of your adversaries, especially in victory.

125. Knowledge has no point unless it can be applied. Those who are puffed up by it are precisely those who are disinclined to live by it.

126. Few are the choices we are given; the sands of time pass quickly by.

127. Hasten not to do good to: no. 13. The man who needs hard experience in order to learn vital lessons.

128. A man in darkness perceives neither his state nor that there is light outside him. But a man in light sees himself and the presence of darkness clearly.

129. A man can bear the weight of his burdens, sorrows or pains twice over if he is given reason for them.

130. A rich man takes out a gold coin from his pocket to help his friend; a poor man takes a similar gold coin from his own pocket to do likewise. Two identical coins; one of much more value than the other.

131. It is not a shame to be a sinner or to err; it is a great shame not to stir yourself to remedy that state.

132. The poverty of love, wisdom or spirit in a man can never be hidden from him who possesses these qualities.

133. It is impossible to love everyone in the same way because everyone is different. But it is entirely possible to love everyone the same amount.

134. It is better that you hold back forgiveness to a man who will never repent of the evil he has inflicted on you. For the value which such a man places upon your forgiveness will always be nought, and he will continue in his perdition in the comfort you have extended to him.

135. A man who is overly jealous over his mate is like a child who will not share his toy.

136. It is said that clothes maketh the man. If that is well said, then even better is the saying that inner clothes maketh the inner man.

137. It is submitted that what God hath joined, let not man put asunder. But if it be God who hath joined, then man is *not able* to put asunder.

138. If you make love to your wife to whom God has not joined you, you are committing adultery against the woman you are not married to, to whom God *has* joined you.

139. You have to build a bridge before you can walk over to a person to tell him where he is wrong. A bridge also enables that person to walk over to you to see why you say you are right.

140. Have you loved with your body, only where your heart is?

141. The permanence of Hell is the permanence of images on recorded tape. Remain in evil, the tape is played. Repent, the tape is erased.

142. Is a hammer good or evil? The answer is in the result: is it a house erected with planks of wood held solidly by nails, or the skull of a person smashed in? Thus is a Christian to evaluate messages from the world of spirit.

143. Your life is shouting so loudly I can't hear what you're saying.

144. Do not wear the fashionable badges of the dissolute, decadent or degenerate, unless you embrace what they stand for. Is beauty to be clothed with ugliness?

145. Rather than the intelligent, athletic and beautiful, the real heroes in life are the slow-witted, disabled and plain, for the former have chosen lives of relative ease. And no persons of either type are to be despised except for fools, and they are to be found in either camp.

146. Are you wise to follow fashion? He with shaved head, skin pierced by tattoos or studs, or clad in the attire of the dark or rebellious, will be presumed to be an ardent devotee of the realms which his appearance depicts.

147. If you violate the rules it is more fortunate if you are apprehended by a general rather than a corporal. A subordinate a mere level above you is liable to be despotic, impatient, and more zealous to boot.

148. Do not be overly curious as to who said an important thing; heed rather what is said. All wisdom is a gift from the Wise One above.

149. Hasten not to do good to: no. 14. Those who need help but who are offended when you offer it. Their pride is more urgent to them than their need.

150. Would you know if you are spiritual? The answer is in but one question: do you find the world a corpse?

151. To command respect you must first earn it, for how can you command what has not presented itself before you?

152. Embarking on something you have deep misgivings about is like giving shelter to a homeless snake. When, bewildered, you ask why it has bitten you, it hisses back, 'You knew I was a snake when you took me in!'

153. Respect is a mutual, two-way quality. But its direction must be heeded: it must first be shown, not by the servant to the master, but by the master to the servant.

154. If a man says, 'There is no God or world of spirit', he is by no means a fool for the mere words. If, however, these words are rooted in his heart he is a fool indeed. For if there were no spirit, that man would be unable to think any thoughts at all, either wise or foolish.

155. Hasten not to do good to: no. 15. The man who is already the recipient of help from other sources, and is keeping it quiet.

156. The only thing that man seems to have learned from history is that man doesn't seem to learn from history.

157. Evil is good inverted. The pentagram commandeered by the witch is holy when oriented upwards to honour God, and the cross of the Christian is evil when oriented downwards to dishonour God.

158. It is said to be an illusion that the other man's grass is always greener. But is it an illusion when your own grass is withered and brown?

159. Blessed is he who gives without remembering; blessed also is he who receives without forgetting.

160. When you read the work of an author, if possible find out his life, because the spirit in his work must always be a reflection of it.

161. 'Faint heart never won fair lady'; but it is often no impediment where the woman is neither fair nor a lady.

162. To deliberately split an infinitive is to grievously inflict a heinous wound upon the English language.

163. Jesus said that the hypocritical Pharisees were whited sepulchres. The more important word is not *whited* but *sepulchres*: corpses posturing as the living.

164. Never a truer word has the atheist spoken than that God is dead. As the world of life is non-existent inside a camera devoid of a film, so is God in the mind of such a man.

165. Riches are a source of true comfort, joy and blessing, if the one who possesses them knows that what he has is freely available to everyone else.

166. Riches are a source of true comfort, joy and blessing, if the one who possesses them is willing to share them with those who lack them.

167. Hasten not to do good to: no. 16. The man who ought first to be helped by his own kin or by the friends who know him well.

168. 'You never get rich working for someone else': a statement which will remain true until men learn to treat others as they themselves would like to be treated.

169. A true story. Valentinius was a wise philosopher in Rome with a reputation for possessing many jewels, and soldiers were despatched to find them. They came across him in the middle of a group of his disciples and proceeded to ransack his dwelling from top to bottom. They searched in vain and left in disgust. Yet Valentinius' jewels were there for all to see.

170. Incompetent people who are hired to run companies show one thing, and that is how accomplished are the mediocre in their powers of persuasion.

171. To most people, God and Santa Claus are identical twins. Both are old men with long white beards, and both are brought to mind only when it is time to turn on the tap of unearned gifts.

172. Human rights are against the interests of people other than those upon whom they are bestowed, unless those rights are reciprocal with human responsibilities.

173. Coincidences are happenstances. If it is by design it is synchronicity. And in all matters of significance in life there is never coincidence.

174. Religion can be summed up as a person having conviction over belief in the unseen. The atheist is a very religious person.

175. Many people desire to preach in order to tell others what they ought to do, but who would not tolerate the reverse.

176. Birds fly with effortless dexterity, fish swim with fluent mastery, lions run as swift as the wind: all these abilities and more outstrip the powers of mortal man. Is then the bird or fish or lion superior to man?

177. Behold the most beautiful sight in the world: a pulchritudinous young maiden of flawless appearance, of delicate and refined features, of ravishing and tender countenance, her breath as rare perfume, and adorned in the graceful attire and in the exquisite scents befitting her maidenhood. Yet still she farts.

178. If you must make judgment over someone or his actions, understand that *what* he is or does is less important than *why* he is as he is or does what he does.

179. The finest teacher you will ever have is not the most eloquent master in the most prestigious place of learning; it is experience. For what are instructions not executed, or theories never tested?

180. Lust is one of the seven deadly sins. If transmuted it becomes one of the seven greatest virtues.

181. Fathers ought never to consider themselves superior to their sons: in times to come in the cycle of life, a father will follow the one who earlier followed *him*.

182. It is a dangerous thing for judgment upon evildoers not to be executed swiftly, for evildoers thereby conclude that the just ascribe no great horror to their crimes and sins.

183. A man who places the Son of God on the same level as Buddha, Confucius, Krishna or Muhammad has not only failed to rise from the spiritual to a taste of the divine, but has yet to rise to the truly spiritual.

184. The greatest illusion a man can be subject to is to be without God and consider himself alive.

185. A father passes on to his son what he received from his own father about how to live life, and his son in turn passes on the same to his own son. The greatest wisdom there is is to find out the point of it.

186. One measure of how deeply people treat each other as they themselves would like to be treated is how far they panic when shortages of the necessities of life come upon them, and how quickly the storehouses of such things are emptied.

187. Unless he is God, a man who says 'Trust me' to someone who knows not his life is demanding what he has no right to receive.

188. Hasten not to do good to: no. 17. Him who is unwilling to pay the cost of obtaining help for himself, who lounges in his chair of comfort while you drop grapes into his mouth.

189. The scientist who prides himself on his implacable disbelief in things unseen is more religious than the scientist whose disbelief in such things is ambivalent.

190. Many an evangelist measures the Love of God by how copious are the blessings He bestows and how scant the pain He inflicts: God made in the image of people who live lives of overabundance and decadent ease.

191. Do not love God less when He brings pain: His pain is temporal – when it ends, recompense begins, and often, the highest blessings are the fruit of the deepest sorrows.

192. If you climb a high mountain and stand on the top you have conquered the mountain. If you stall just short of the top, the mountain has conquered you.

193. You do not start to learn when you enter school; you start to learn when you leave it.

194. We live in a world of instant coffee, instant entertainment, and instant gratification. A clue as to why love, friendship, trust, patience, and fortitude are rare in people?

195. Enlightened societies? For every teacher in America or Britain who aspires to teach children, there are twenty children who are disinclined to learn.

196. God always answers the prayer of a sincere man – without exception. Frequently His answer is 'No' or 'Wait'.

197. A person adorned in a fragrant scent is not necessarily a fragrant person.

198. Hasten not to do good to: no. 18. People you have already helped but their subsequent actions make for a continuation of their predicament.

199. Though a man may be a mute, when he ventures out among his fellows his demeanour and attire speak a language powerful enough to make up for that disability.

200. I am not offended when someone greets me and confesses he has forgotten my name. Better my name be lost to his memory than my face.

201. A woman of exceptionally beautiful features knows it. If she ignores her gift, she has stepped on the path to becoming an exceptionally beautiful person.

202. Not a wise saying but a truth which no one knows: when a killer despatches his victim, he knows not that his victim is awake, close by, and beholding his every move; or, in the case of a child or other overly frightened soul who is whisked away, his guardian spirit.

203. Peter said, 'Silver and gold have I none; but what I have I give thee: take up thy bed and walk.' The prosperity evangelist says, 'Silver and gold thou hast; what thou hast, give to God through me, and He may grant thee to take up thy bed and walk.'

204. Hasten not to do good to: no. 19. Him whose cup is already overflowing with goodness already extended to him.

205. The most intolerant are those who force on others the tolerances of political correctness.

206. Do not live up to others' expectations, unless that other is your God. Do others care to live up to *your* expectations?

207. Many years have I dwelt among a people whose forebears conquered other races in the name of their god and enlightenment. And how many are my fellows whose enlightened state exceeds that of the Native American?

208. Perfume: for adornment or for concealment?

209. How to confuse a space traveller long seasoned by journey-
ing through the constellations shining gloriously in the
heavens: present before him the likes of attention-seeking
celebrities on earth, and refer to them as stars.

210. When a man spits venom over his neighbour's failings, is
he saying less about his neighbour than he is about himself?

211. Which has the more value – respect from someone who fears
you, or respect from someone in whom fear of you is absent?

212. The presence of the organ of elimination serves to keep men
humble: it is an organ shared with the beasts. It is also an
organ shared by both the king and his servant, Venus de
Milo and the Hunchback, the famous and the obscure.

213. When a man prays, is he marvelling at the eloquence of his
own words rather than listening to the response of his God?

214. How to hijack the English language: ascribe to the
condition of homosexuality a word signifying happy and
joyful; and generate offence when someone tries to use the
word 'gay' with its proper meaning.

215. A maths lesson: proportionality is the measure of how
things change in unison. The multiplicity of a man's
possessions and his enjoyment of any given one of their
number are in inverse proportion.

216. Jesus said, 'Man shall not live by bread alone.' The rich
respond by wanting jam on it.

217. Hasten not to do good to: no. 20. Anyone from whom you
expect to receive back.

218. *Modesty*: a tasteful concealment of what would be shameful
and vulgar if on open display. Pray tell me the meaning of the
scant clothing on a brazen woman being described as only just
covering her modesty. For 'modesty', read 'sex organs'.

219. A soul cannot be killed; it can only be transferred elsewhere. Were you confusing the soul with the body it happened to live in at the time?

220. A Muslim woman in a burqa is making a statement: 'My soul is possessed by my husband and he hides my beauty as a child hides his toy from other children.'

221. Ponder the great number of spirit guides who are Native Americans. This shows but one thing: the love which these souls have for those who afflicted them extends beyond the grave.

222. Never refer to him as a joyrider; he is a thief and a lowlife who destroys the joy of the car's owner, riding roughshod over it with grief.

223. A youth overly enjoying the pleasures of life regards the baubles he gazes upon as jewels. Eyes enamoured by glitter and sparkle.

224. Seven wives and a hundred lovers. But the only woman I have never committed adultery with is the one to whom God joined me when He created us together.

225. Hasten not to do good to: no. 21. Anyone who you have reason to fear would trumpet your good deed to the world.

226. If you encounter a person, do you not ask after his father and mother? Then consider the Christian who encounters Jesus: whom it is he asks after? The Father and the Holy Spirit. Over the centuries men have killed over such a concoction of a family unit.

227. Trying to hide your true self from one with spiritual eyes is like trying to hide your bones from an X-ray machine.

228. When introduced to a plain or fat woman of no obvious appeal, praise her attractive eyes or her beautiful smile. But keep your tongue if you cannot do so in sincerity.

229. The rich eat rich food and the poor eat poor food. But the contents of their bowels end up in the same place. And you can't tell whose is whose.

230. The Son of God stands at the door of a person's life and knocks. Many are the people whose doors are shut fast. Their hearts are bolted tight by the pleasures of life more firmly than handles and locks long rusted.

231. Does a very rich man earn his salary? The answer is the word 'earn': this little word signifies the deserving of a reward which is in proportion to the work done by the man to attain it.

232. A criminal dies peaceful, happy and content, having covered his tracks right to the end. All his friends were louses: not one of them in his long seventy-year life was ever good enough to warn him about the Akashic records.

233. Listen first to what a man has to tell you excitedly about himself, rather than express what you are excited to tell him about yourself.

234. He who has no fear of the unknown after death may have reason to regret his untrammelled boldness.

235. How can you receive or even hear a reply from God if you're hogging the conversation?

236. How to deal with the Christian neurosis of seeing demons around every astral corner: throw the Christian a challenge made by Einstein by the saying 'Is the universe friendly or unfriendly?'

237. In adversity, is it strength that is the first to fail; or the will to live?

238. A rich man on earth compared to a poor man in Heaven is like a man possessing an ornate gilt chest containing a thousand baubles bedecked with tinsel, compared to a man in whose hand is a single gold nugget.

239. Hasten not to do good to: no. 22. Someone who doesn't want your help, and you've got it into your head your mission is to save him.

240. Giving sincere respect to someone undeserving of it is like giving gold to an idler. A paradox: credit for him who gives and discredit for him who receives.

241. A child who has a doll cherishes it; a child who has a hundred dolls treasures none.

242. How fierce is your love for God? Do you embrace His wrath more fervently than His kindness?

243. Is a people overabundant in wealth and ease? Pay regard to its children: are they its oppressors, the tail wagging the dog?

244. Do you want to partake in prayer which is not a vain exercise? Then talk less and listen more.

245. 1. You who possess a spiritual gift: give freely the benefit of it and do not sell it. If it is your living, sell only the costs incurred.

246. 2. You who possess a spiritual gift of healing: sell it not, neither your costs.

247. The materialist wants the good things within this life; the spiritualist wants the good things beyond this life.

248. Hasten not to do good to: no. 23. The person attended by deep sorrow, but who remains in the pit of despair and refuses to rise out of it.

249. A child still unruly at five years and Pandora's box tell the same tale: though you try with all your might, you cannot retrieve what has escaped to fly away.

250. Three prostitutes: she who sells her body; she who grows rich by selling her beauty; and he who merchandises the spiritual gifts given him by God.

251. Do not overly protest that unpunished criminals or the undeserving rich who die contented demonstrate an unfair world. Such people awake to what is an utter surprise to them, and it is not a continuation of the fortune they died with.

252. In a free society, boredom is not a reaction to dull surroundings; it is simply a symptom of an unexercised mind.

253. Drunkenness is a revealer of secrets. The destructive violence, or the exuberant merriment, of an inebriated man is merely the aroused state of what already couches in his heart.

254. In the history of religion multitudes of people have been persecuted for foolishness' sake.

255. A fool is a man with two organs having holes for eliminating waste, one in the usual place and the other in front of his face.

256. Nature is a good teacher of morals, dispensing with the need for words: note young women who self-consciously and surreptitiously tug at their short skirts in the street to try to make them longer.

257. Hasten not to do good to: no. 24. The parasite whose habit is to feed off and drain your beneficence.

258. Victim or fighter? You can't be both of them, but you can choose to be one of them.

259. Spiders love bored minds; they cannot spin webs around minds that won't stay still.

260. You can bet your bottom dollar that in his addiction a gambler will wager his last coin

261. You don't receive a martyr's grace until you become a martyr.

262. In the aftermath of a battle, the victor is not he who has lost fewer men but he who has established the principles on which he fought.

263. Better a prosperous person be charged a reasonable sum for a service rendered him, than he receive it free of cost.

264. Hollywood: the desperate struggle of many an attention-seeking mortal to eke out, at obscene expense, a few extra years of wrinkle-free skin, oblivious to the gathering wrinkles of vanity and self-importance in his soul.

265. Yes, the Negro has a black face. Those who have reviled and enslaved him may have a white face, but they have a black heart.

266. Do not look askance at the child who keeps a threadbare doll or at the man who continues to drive an old, battered car. It's not the doll or car which is the beneficiary, but the soul who is learning the meaning of enduring love.

267. If you try to buy friendship all you will ever get is cheap junk.

268. Take heed that if you are going up in the world you are not going down in the spirit.

269. Telling people to pray to God can be incautious; people are already in the habit of listening to themselves talk without being interrupted.

270. Hasten not to do good to: no. 25. Those who feign need and poverty then turn your munificence against you.

271. Charity begins at home. True charity spreads beyond home.

272. The way to judge a sinner deep in his sin is to ascertain his direction: is he descending deeper into his sin or striving to raise himself out from it?

273. 'Nothing personal,' explains the tyrant oppressing his subjects. Too true: there was a time when a person was who he used to be.

274. The pain suffered by the victim of a murderer is often exceeded by that of those who survive him.

275. A loose woman complains that men treat her as a piece of meat. However, a man salivates more quickly over a juicy steak, and his stomach more readily digests such a delicacy, than it does ideals of beauty or love.

276. The gossip or rumour monger blames her friends for listening.

277. Lateral thinking: which came first, the chicken or the egg? The cock.

278. Take heart, thou who art distressed over an unjust, politically correct society. Though obscure and few, there are indeed those who flout the rules for the sake of what is morally correct.

279. In the wrong place at the wrong time? Do not hasten to conclude it a tragic misfortune. For you know not what lies behind the event in spirit.

280. Humility for the musical virtuoso: let him eschew the adulation and applause at the conclusion of his performance. Let him step down from the podium and join the audience in applause for the one who wrote the music.

281. Don't give up a bad habit and grit your teeth; it will return and fill the space vacated. Give up a bad habit and replace it with a better habit.

282. Christians all want to enter the Kingdom of Heaven. And they all want to be the kings or the priests.

283. The atheist cosmonaut who returned from a trip into space reported that he did not see God up there. Yes he did, the same as you and I do every time we look up into a starry night sky.

284. Hasten not to do good to: no. 26. Those who milk currency out of wallowing in misfortune and enjoy the attention and sympathy it yields them.

285. Proof there is such a thing as a Group Soul: no. 1. Walk down the street or among a gathering of people, play Mozart or Beethoven on a music player at a loud volume, then note the reaction of the crowd. Case rested.

286. God feeds birds, but He doesn't drop worms into their nests.

287. Do the loudest fashions dress a soul with the least to say?

288. Be a sounding board for another's woes, but do not be an emotional waste-paper basket.

289. Mathematics lesson: in satisfying public demand, the quality of the works of an artist can be expected to vary in inverse proportion to the number of such works he churns out hastily in the shortest space of time.

290. A snare is a trap leading to freedom lost, disguised as a gate leading to freedom gained. Sex is a trap, and sex without love a snare.

291. Three things whose beauty is the equal of that of a woman: a butterfly flitting among flowers in the sun; a copse of trees in a rustic landscape; and a glorious sunset with tranquil clouds edged in fiery gold.

292. Proof there is such a thing as a Group Soul: no. 2. A person indulges an obnoxious habit among his fellows. Many are discomfited and offended – he hasn't asked permission – yet no one tells or asks him to desist. Welcome to the world of the smoker, and case rested.

293. Many weeds are flowers whose beauty has not yet been discovered.

294. Hasten not to do good to: no. 27. Those whose motivation and confidence to do good to themselves without leaning on others is thereby dispensed with.

295. As a caterpillar is a butterfly-in-waiting, so is a sinner a saint-in-waiting.

296. You are curious to know who wrote a wise saying? Is your
      attention drawn to the beggar who has stumbled upon a
      sparkling precious stone in the dirt and has held it up to
      show everyone – or to the jewel?

297. Contentment is when you've arrived and you want to stay.
      Discontentment is when your feet don't agree.

298. Why did you allow it to happen, God? An answer: Why
      did you cause it to happen by insisting on your freedom to
      ignore me?

299. The path to God traces its course through a succession of
      cities, each of which is possessed of a particular illusion.
      One city bears the curious name of Evangelical Christianity.
      Its own illusion is to cause those who arrive there to think
      they are at the very end of their journey.

300. Miracles are bad for you when God can speak to you
      without them.

301. Free will is like a large circular pool. You can splash around,
      dive and choose any direction and manner you want to move
      in. But eventually you reach the water's edge.

302. Religious language of the Christian who professes to know
      God personally: 'Do you know the Lord Jesus?' Would you
      ever approach Mr Jones and ask him, 'How is the
      Mrs Jones?'

303. Proof there is such a thing as a Group Soul: no. 3. Stroll
      down the street and mark the women, uncomfortable in their
      low-slung jeans which they constantly try to pull above their
      buttocks, or the shoes which cripple their feet. Case rested.

304. A dark shadow to a fearful man is a solid black monster.

305. Hasten not to do good to: no. 28. Those who in response
      to your kindness turn into pests by coming to you again
      and again.

306. If you pray to God for a miracle, He might agree with you and send you the plan telling you how to obtain it.

307. How to tell if it is your true soulmate you're courting: romance is redundant.

308. Loving a second person does not mean you love the first person less.

309. 'I love you so much,' intones the person gazing at the beautiful butterfly he has netted and put in a jar.

310. You entered this world without clothes, teeth, hair or control over your bowels. And that is probably how you will leave it.

311. You desire to teach the world the deep things you know? Is it to benefit the world, or to dazzle it?

312. The first action of a newborn infant is to wail and void its bowels. Its reaction at entering a world far inferior to the one it has just left behind?

313. 'Don't venture outside: the air's toxic!' entreats the Christian in his cocoon. Someone had told him the outside was dark and labelled 'occult'.

314. The Roman Catholic, the Protestant, the evangelical, the Jehovah's Witness, the Jew and the Muslim all die, each fully expecting to receive a ringing divine endorsement that his religion is the right one and all the others are wrong. His expectation will be met with but one question: 'What have you done with your life that you can show me?'

315. When confronting an adversary, fix your gaze into his eyes. For the eyes are the portals whence he exercises his power over you, and yours over him.

316. Hasten not to do good to: no. 29. Those who regard you as a generous individual whose money tap is endless.

317. If you could see inside the mind of a praying man, you would often behold the man in the pulpit and God in the pew.

318. Take care to live honestly before your children: their eyes make them great imitators – they copy what they see, and are often deaf to what they hear.

319. Why are you affected by your rejection by others who do not subscribe to your belief in things unseen? If they are digging a grave, it is their own.

320. There is a man more blind than he who will not see. And that is he who has seen who will not see.

321. A jealous person who inhibits his beloved from spreading love beyond the confines of their bond together is like someone who seriously expects to toss a pebble into a still pond without creating ripples on its surface.

322. The man who is adamant in his refusal to believe in life after death will continue to cling zealously to that state in the life after his death.

323. The best preaching is living, not preaching.

324. Hasten not to do good to: no. 30. The spendthrifts who quickly drain you of everything you give them and have nothing left.

325. The famous healer or evangelist says, 'Do not give me the glory which belongs to God.' Fat chance: he has already appropriated it by the ostentation of his display.

326. A man might refrain from uttering words of thanks for the kind deed you have rendered him, but his eyes will speak his gratitude, or lack of it.

327. Love is like ripples on a pond: no part of the water's surface remains still. Not one around can escape being affected.

328. A church surrounded by tombstones: is the outside of the church a picture of life inside it?

329. Poor spelling, punctuation, grammar and diction. Adequate communication? Perhaps. Excellence and refinement? Not a chance.

330. How a lecherous man counts a line of women: 2, 4, 6, 8, 10, 12… Six!

331. Is a tattoo on a person's skin an embellishment or a disfigurement?

332. If people became more honest in their outward appearance, would the makers of white wedding dresses go out of business?

333. Hasten not to good to: no. 31. Those who lavish praise on you for your aid – and who promptly forget they have been rescued.

334. 'You don't listen to a word I say,' she complains to her wayward teenager. This mother's probably wrong; her off-spring is listening intently – not to the words of her mouth, but to those of her life.

335. They say cameras never lie. True, but people who operate cameras do.

336. Sometimes the greatest journey in life is traversing the distance between two people.

337. How to make a church a more honest place: put the pews and pulpit on the same level.

338. 'Sow a $1,000 seed and God will answer your need,' assures the evangelist. The goodness of God measured by money. Bought, sold, marketed, packaged.

339. How to give a fundamentalist Christian a nervous break-down: present the evidence for extraterrestrial races and ask him in whose image they are made.

340. The judgment of a spiritually wise man is like the waves of the sea against the rocks of the shore. The water finds every crack, and no secret crevice can hide from it.

341. One sin in an otherwise unblemished life is like one ink spot on a white sheet of paper.

342. A celebrity whose habit is to reinvent herself by changing her image elicits one entreaty: please show us which of these presentations is the real you!

343. Fear a quiet captain rather than a loud general.

344. Hasten not to do good to: no. 32. Those whom you help, and who think thereby that what you have is theirs to claim.

345. Can a crowd show forth virtue in the human heart? Is not sweetness of taste rather to be found in the individual apple?

346. Christians don't listen when Jesus said to His disciples, 'I will make you fishers of men.' To their ears He said, 'I will make you trawlers of men,' and they think to save every fish in the ocean.

347. A judge muses to himself that he has the power to acquit or to condemn; what he has is the power to judge with right judgment.

348. He who frequents places of entertainment is someone who escapes there to drown out the thoughts and voices within him.

349. A drug taker is a selfish coward, afraid of and avoiding real life when it becomes mundane. And also greedy for illegitimate and instant short cuts to an experience of nirvana not earned.

350. First love her; then understand her.

351. If you consider you have a head on your shoulders wiser than other people's, unless they are children, desist from telling them.

352. Opportunities are courteous, temptations impudent. The first ring the doorbell, the second lean on it.

353. Quarrels would peter out quickly if the fault lay only on one side.

354. The wise speak because they have something to say; fools because they have to say something.

355. When you get to know a plain or even ugly woman, but one with a good heart, her face becomes beautiful. And the reverse: outward beauty sours for the want of such a heart.

356. If you try to chase two hares at the same time you will catch neither.

357. The secret of looking younger than your years is to take along your youthful ways with you as you grow older instead of abandoning your ways to the oblivion of the past.

358. If you allow everyone to walk all over you, you will become a carpet.

359. A hidden deception of modern life: two companies compete for your custom; both are owned by the same parent.

360. Don't build a house by dutifully following everyone's advice. If you do you will never get it straight.

361. Hasten not to do good to: no. 33. The person whose friends and acquaintances would form a queue at your door hoping for the same bounty.

362. Ignorance is less of a shame than not bothering to find out.

363. To test a man's maturity give him authority.

364. Take heart, plain lady: try as you might, unless your body or your face is misshapen, it is simply impossible for you to be ugly.

365. Learn the rules in your times of study; apply them by experience.

366. Don't curse the dark – light a candle.

367. People are lions at telling you how to surmount your difficulties.

368. When children run out of something to do, beware: mischief beckons.

369. Kindness can be praised by the mute, heard by the deaf, and read by the blind.

370. In an unequal union, the inferior boasts of it and the superior bows his head or blushes.

371. A miracle moves the prejudiced in vain. The testimony of the eyes is insufficient to break the locks of a closed mind. In six months the miracle will be denied, reinterpreted or forgotten.

372. If you want an apple, climb the tree.

373. Hasten not to do good to: no. 34. Him already the recipient of an abundance of fortune and comfort and is in the midst of a temporary difficulty.

374. Till death us do part? Many marriages expire almost before they've begun.

375. Work hard and play hard. And hate hard and love hard.

376. Think twice before you refuse a gift. You may disappoint the giver who is learning how to give, or him whose recompense for sacrifice is deep joy.

377. If you don't get a grip on yourself, life and people will get their own grip on you.

378. If everyone were good at maths, would gambling become a rare pursuit?

379. Do not be hasty writing off the old person who appears to mutter to himself. How do you know but that he is not communing with those he will soon be meeting?

380. A man who swears fails badly to convince; he who swears to God fails even more badly. He whose yes is yes and his no is no might perchance convince.

381. A hidden deception of modern life: all the companies which make widgets boast they are of superior quality. Where, pray, are the inferior widgets that the superior widgets are superior to?

382. Never take your eyes away from those of a snarling dog baring its fangs. Show him neither your fear nor your back. To a dog, your rear quarters and your fear share the same bed of weakness.

383. The timid flee from monsters that aren't there.

384. To a fearful man the disaster will most definitely come to pass.

385. The thing about a lukewarm person is that you can't tell whether he was once hot or once cold.

386. Hasten not to do good to: no. 35. Anyone whose display of gratitude is liable to engender in you a sense of pride and self-importance.

387. A terrible choice for a young woman to have to make: a tall, handsome and virile poor man of twenty-five; or a short, podgy and unhealthy rich man of sixty-five. Not so terrible, though, if the latter is ninety-five instead of sixty-five.

388. A deeper truth for spiritualists: if your spirit guide does not believe in the Son of God and you do, there will come a time when your roles are reversed, but provided that you lack not the greatest humility and respect.

389. Parents neither create nor do they own their offspring. They are merely surrogates, boats on the sea which their children are dropped into at a convenient time and leave again when they have learned to swim.

390. If the devil appears to look after his own, he has an agenda.

391. Orthodox Christianity is like Chapter One of a car maintenance manual. Christians are proud of their ability to change the oil and inflate tyres, constantly repeating such tasks, posturing as experts. Engine overhauls are God's job.

392. Bored people need exercise. Give a cat in an empty room a mouse to play with. The mouse will not be bored or unexercised for long.

393. Accomplished politicians are those who have perfected the art of doing something in full view of people at the same time as convincing them they're doing the opposite.

394. 'Buy it now before it sells out! A better home! A better car! A better style of fashion!' Better than what?

395. Animals are held up as examples to the failings of humans. But observe the great number of animals which never clean up their mess after them, which are heedless of the bodily waste they deposit in the open, and those which never respond to the cries of one of their number in distress.

396. Dogs are often seen doing it in the street in the full view of passers-by. The same is true of many of the inebriated in a city centre at night.

397. You can be absolutely certain when a politician is telling the truth: that is when his lips are at rest. Even then you might notice his eyes twitching.

398. Hasten not to do good to: no. 36. Anyone who burdens you with guilt if you procrastinate over your decision to aid him.

399. The truly respectful man has previously learned a prior lesson: humility.

400. A liar is a man with a God-shaped hole in his heart and a devil-shaped hole on his face.

401. A temptress is a woman with a God-shaped hole in her heart and a devil-shaped hole between her legs.

402. The young woman is getting ready to go out nightclubbing, drinking and dancing with her friends. She scratches her head at the goodwill of her grandmother. 'Why? Because, my dear, that's all you have.'

403. A king and a garbage collector need each other to the same degree, and both take good advantage of each other.

404. *Sign of an oppressive society: six squad cars with horns blaring, two Black Marias, three police dogs, the searchlight from a chopper overhead, an ambulance – and two drunks fighting.*

405. A little judicious decoration with cosmetics brings out her beauty; a little too much and her beauty is diminished.

406. Is it right or wrong to hate? Is your hatred directed at a legitimate object and governed by the constraints of wisdom and control?

407. Communication is vital for a good marriage or friendship. You will wait in vain for iron filings near an iron bar to form a pattern around it unless you first magnetise the bar.

408. A poppy in a field. A child sees a pretty flower. A drug taker sees opium; and if also a dealer, the field full of them, and the prospect of a fat wallet.

409. The dream of a prostitute is her next client's money.

410. Voltaire on his deathbed and espying a flickering candle: 'The flames already?' Most others will think they've arrived to see a fireworks display, and will not be disabused of that notion until the moment their flesh is touched.

411. A good cure for loneliness: stroll into the countryside and behold the butterflies, the birds, the trees, the flowers, the rustling brook: all these are the handiwork of loving spirits who are present to care for them.

412. A favourite passage of Scripture: the woman caught in the very act of adultery. I am that woman: I prostituted the talents God gave me, I was discovered, I was accused, I was tried, I was convicted, and I was forgiven.

413. I am an outlaw reformed, but not my former partner. He was freed by a lawman who ran out of jail cell space. I was sent to serve time in a cell by a judge who had the power to execute me.

414. Dwelling with a contentious woman is like filling your spoon with gravel.

415. The rich young store owner to Jesus: 'I have never cheated any of my customers.' His reply: 'One thing you lack: let your $9.99s always be $10.00s.'

416. The more you know, the more you realise how little you know.

417. How to impose an unpopular scheme on people: first present to them an outrageous version, put it to a vote, lose, then introduce the intended milder scheme, saying, 'We have listened to your voice, O people.'

418. A hidden deception of modern life: 'Buy now! Reduced from $30 to a ridiculous $10 – an absolute bargain!' Its true price was only ever $10.

419. If at first you don't succeed, don't stop praying.

420. The heart of a judge may be moved by much he learns about your life that commands his honour, respect and compassion. But is his hand moved away from sanctioning the penalty for your misdeed?

421. Hit someone hard over the head next time you see him reading his fortune in the daily paper. Either way he'll see stars which aren't there.

422. The laughter of a little child playing with lambs among the flowers and trees of a sunlit meadow is purer than the crystal waters of the sparkling brook which trickle past.

423. Don't be the hero and dive unthinkingly into a stranger's life to help him out of his difficulty. There is a species of caterpillar which struggles to emerge from its cocoon. Help it out and it dies. Its struggle gives it the strength to survive.

424. Some people in whose lives misfortune and pain are unknown are truly delightful and enchanting persons. But touch them with the sting of common experience...

425. A people is corrupted by its leaders in imperceptibly small steps. Larger steps and they would notice. Same as temptations of the devil, really.

426. Do not overly burden your children. They have ten years of a light heart and seventy to follow of a heart made heavy.

427. A man's life is ordained to be one of sacrifice. He sacrifices his principles and honour, or his want of them: his innocence or his guilt.

428. 'There is no intelligent life outside my world,' announces the ant scientist who has never left the confines of the ants' nest at the bottom of the garden.

429. Man is made in God's image, so there can be no superior non-human life. So muses the Christian, his eyes shut in thought, while a spaceship hovers above him and a magnificent, huge crop circle is being formed in front of him.

430. A frog surrounded by flies does not venture to satisfy its hunger if its source of food stays motionless. It will die in its want of sustenance. The same for Christians surrounded by dogmatic creeds and sclerotic beliefs.

431. The three true classes in society: workers (upper class), the ailing or work-shy (middle class), and the idle rich (lower class).

432. The woman hiding an onion under her handkerchief at her dearly departed's funeral knows not that the dead who have chosen to hang around before going into the light have X-ray vision.

433. Child abuse? How about divorce (abuse of the right of a child to have two parents)? Sex education (abuse of the right of a child to be taught that sex involves love as well as biology)? Celebrities (abuse of the right of a child to enjoy heroes and role models devoid of sexual pressure)?

434. Christians think their belief in sins forgiven sufficient to ensure them a place next to God in Heaven. However, Heaven is a like an airport: it has a waiting area.

435. Do people talk about the weather because it's the only thing that changes in their lives?

436. Better a dinner of herbs where love is than a stalled ox and hatred therewith.

437. Loneliness is the lot of someone yet to learn the meaning of solitude.

438. Alexander the Great, who conquered huge tracts of territory and subdued many peoples, was himself felled – in his youth by a microscopic virus.

439. 'Why are you taking so long to answer my prayer, God?' 'Maybe when I do something, son, I like to do it properly.'

440. Don't envy the idle: their lifestyle comes at a cost. Do you, too, want to be fat and ailing?

441. What most atheists are really doing is not doubting God's reality but overthrowing an image of God which is unwelcome in their hearts.

442. Being old may be a state of decrepitude, but is it not also an achievement?

443. No fire like passion, stranglehold like hatred, snare like delusion, nor torment like craving.

444. Never presume that he who utters a wise saying is himself as wise as his words. He is as challenged by the saying as are his fellows.

445. 'I believe in God,' you say. That's good, so does the devil: if you don't believe, you're a fool, an idiot, or you lack perception: one of the three.

446. What you look for in people you will most probably find.

447. In the midst of great suffering it is not always a shame to disbelieve in God. Such a man is in a box devoid of light, its lid clamped shut.

448. From the heart of a young woman armed with a calculator is offered utter devotion towards any 95-year-old rich man, however decrepit his condition.

449. The life of a rich, famous, successful and admired man speaks volumes of worldly wisdom and knowledge. But of the ways of spirit he probably has nothing to say.

450.   You want to go to Heaven when you die. Is that to see the place, or meet God and the people who live there?

451.   The best way to win people round to your way of thinking is to meet them on the ground of their way of thinking.

452.   If you dress up a wolf as a sheep it is still a wolf. So are the bad schemes of a people's leaders when given cosmetic changes to make them look good.

453.   Love comes out of the worst hovels and hate out of the richest mansions.

454.   You are hid in the nest of God's love high on the cliff, and none can reach you though they try. But one thought and you can remove yourself at any time.

455.   Children grow up into adults. And the world is full of seventy-year-old children and not a few ten-year-old adults.

456.   The day will dawn when war will cease among men left to their own devices. It will be when their hands are chopped off.

457.   You have sinned against your God. Is He the more angry because you have offended Him, or because you have offended yourself?

458.   Taking on a loose woman is like trying to mould a pile of dry sand into the shape of a cake, much less trying to ice the damn thing.

459.   If you, a common worker, are stormed at by a superior for a minor misdemeanour, take it in good grace: the burdens which weigh upon a superior are likely to be heavier than any which weigh upon an underling.

460.   Gandhi: 'An eye for an eye only makes the whole world blind.'

461.   The spirit of keeping up with the Joneses is alive and well when, in a street of a hundred families, your life is not worth living because you have only the second-biggest car.

462. Circumstances influence your choices; they do not necessarily determine them.

463. The dazzling film 'star' and a lowly caterpillar have much in common. Both are destined to be transformed into butterflies so beautiful that by comparison they are presently both grubs.

464. The strongest and tallest man compared to the weakest and shortest angel is like the biggest ant compared to the smallest elephant.

465. The greatest hatred towards God is not an antagonistic disposition but a self-sufficient indifference.

466. The self-centred child wants his parents to come to him in his chair of comfort when he calls. Take heed you do not treat your God like that.

467. The most beautiful caterpillar in the world will always be inferior to the plainest butterfly. O plain woman with a good heart, exult in your destiny!

468. Perfect love is never being the centre of your own universe.

469. The sweet sound of an American evangelist: 'Of course, you do not express love to God merely in material ways such as giving money. Oh no, there are many other ways: you can also give your jewellery, houses, land, bequests…'

470. The idle and lethargic really do love activity and work: they love it so much they watch it in comfort every day on TV.

471. If God is a male Father, where do women come from?

472. The obedience of a slave devoid of love for his master is like the cold light of the winter's sun.

473. What matters in life are your choices, not your successes. A wrong choice means success in vain.

474. Many of those who seek and fail to find conclude that their quest was in vain rather than that they set out in blindness.

475. When you are indecisive over an important issue, is it because you are at a loss to know the right direction to go in, or are you employing a device to avoid going in it?

476. It is fortunate Jesus was not born in America or Britain: the social services department would long ago have put Mary's baby up for adoption.

477. God is perfect in His ways, making no mistakes. A person makes no mistakes only if he is dead.

478. It is rash to trust the promises of a renewed world of peace and prosperity uttered by a sage who ignores the war and poverty in the unrenewed hearts of men.

479. Is loneliness a state of being without people, or being asleep to the realisation that you are surrounded by your true family?

480. If he lives with an incompatible woman as his wife, an Englishman's home is his sandcastle.

481. Dealing with an untruthful man is harder than trying to nail jelly to a wall.

482. If a man is that jealous over what his wife might get up to with the milk delivery man while he's at work, he'd better get a cow.

483. Do not dive in haste into new discoveries, or you may find yourself following in the footsteps of an impetuous child rushing to cross an unfamiliar street in heavy traffic.

484. Making a mistake is OK; repeating a mistake is maybe OK; repeating a mistake over and over is not OK.

485. Many value what they have in terms of its superiority to that of their neighbours. When their neighbours play catch-up, then what they have is drained of its appeal.

486. If you have missed a flower on the path of your life because you ran too fast, you will pass it again.

487. A religious cult isn't defined by its small size in a corner and few adherents. Forget Mormons or Jehovah's Witnesses; look at churches much bigger.

488. Heaven to me is flowers which never shrivel, children who never grow old, summer which never turns to winter, and my beloved whose devotion dieth not.

489. A stopped watch or a capricious child? At least you can rely on the watch to tell the right time, if only twice a day.

490. Mistakes are great teachers: they are their own means to show that it is not mistakes which matter but why you made them.

491. People hate being preached at. The important word in this statement is the one with the fewest letters.

492. The greater miracle? A cripple made to walk again, or a soul rehabilitated from criminality?

493. Your words have power. Repeat the mantra 'I am a sinner', and it will come to be. Repeat the mantra 'I am the child of a sinless God', and that also will come to be.

494. Wonder not at the man who withdraws from the throng into solitude. Away from the noise of the throng you can discern the bliss of his peace.

495. The vanity of a man who would be famous: see, the whole world worships you. And the whole world is but a single grain of sand on the shifting dunes of the seashore on the edge of the swirling ocean of the heavens.

496. A tattoo on a man or woman is like graffiti on the work of a great artist.

497. It must be difficult for gossips to get together to wag their tongues. How do they manage to get their rumours in edgeways?

498. God forgives you instantly, but if you do not truly rue your action you are not ready to procure His gift.

499. The jealous man expresses interest only in love from his beloved, but the true lover watches out for the interest of his beloved.

500. Precious words from Mother Teresa: 'You will see the Love of God in the smile of a child.'

501. Those who know the least profess the most.

502. A woman's love is like a flower. Fail to water it and it shrivels.

503. A spendthrift wife confirming the changeability of some women's minds: she spends her own money, then starts on her husband's. No, no: she spends her husband's money, then starts on her own.

504. Fundamentalists bicker over their concepts of God as a trinity, and the Holy Ghost as a ghost or a person. None thinks to ask where is the Mother of the Son at the side of His Father.

505. Many politicians are grown-up children. A nursery should feel very proud to be asked to rent out to them one of its rooms for a conference.

506. If you could see into the mind of a devious and corrupt man you would see his conscience and his devil making sordid deals.

507. The Love of God is tough love.

508. The Jehovah's Witnesses are right, so the others are wrong; the Mormons are right, so the others are wrong; the Muslims are right, so the others are wrong. And God is right, so the others are wrong.

509. Love can hurt the one who loves.

510. People are in a race of life measuring progress in terms of speed, time and distance. It is not a race partaken in by those who are spiritual.

511. In the animal kingdom the male is often the brighter coloured, the female the plainer. Medallion man, don't kid yourself!

512. It is of grave concern to social workers in Britain to see young boys in stores buying condoms and shaving cream. Not long ago, boys didn't start shaving until they were older.

513. *Opportunity*: the most important key word to success in a non-spiritual world. The passport to fleecing your customers, fiddling your company, making out with your neighbour's spouse, keeping for yourself what you find on the ground...

514. *Choice*: one small key word in life with an incalculable result.

515. If Hell is infinite, then the Love of God is finite, ending where Hell begins. But if the Love of God is infinite, then it begins where Hell ends.

516. Don't keep agreeing with your argumentative wife; you might make her start to think she must be wrong.

517. Though a good father chastises his son with grievous blows, his blows are not those of an enemy.

518. An unbeliever seeks to prove an inconvenient proposition wrong; a wise man exerts himself to prove it right.

519. Alcohol is a depressant that depressed people take to alleviate depression.

520. Devils may have blazing red eyes and breathe the fire of dragons, but they have no power over you except that which you give them.

521. The face of a wrinkled old woman might not be an oil painting, but if you look more closely it has depth and is much more interesting.

522. How is my capricious teenage daughter going to act today? I haven't a clue; all I know is I feel safer believing the weather forecast for two weeks hence.

523. If Jesus upheld tithing your money, He would say, 'Freely you have received, freely give 10% of it.'

524. Trying to force understanding into an unwilling or oblivious person is like trying to force food into a full stomach.

525. Absence makes the heart grow fonder – or, if bereft of love, colder.

526. A recipe. Take a proper Christian religion, add spiritual awareness, place in the oven, heat and take out again. What you have is a proper Christian.

527. People rarely make good use of dating agencies; the type of men or women they imagine meeting don't need one.

528. Lofty language imparted from inspired lips in public prayer is not to be interpreted as arising from a lofty spirit.

529. Two unfortunate men: one relieved of the contents of his wallet by a man with a gun; the other by a spendthrift wife.

530. If you want to go through the motions in your life, take up religion. If you want your motions to be profitable as you go through your life, take up faith.

531. Satanists are stupid people. Do they really expect their hero to treat them better than he has taught them to treat everyone else?

532. It's not necessarily a reflection on you if he does not accept you. If he doesn't accept himself, how can he?

533. Excitement, feverish bustle and noisy activity: necessary endeavours to meet the demands of one's life, or devices to appear important?

534. Excitement, feverish bustle and noisy activity: necessary endeavours to meet the demands of one's life, or devices to mask a lack of tranquillity and serenity?

535. If at first you don't succeed it may be because it's worth fighting for.

536. Christian, you consider yourself a saint. But are you saintly?

537. White men made one promise to the Native Americans which they kept: they promised to relieve them of their land. And therein lies the clue to the name Wall Street.

538. Conquer yourself, and truly, the world lies at your feet.

539. You don't get bonuses with the wages of sin, but you do get severance pay.

540. Better to give than to lend.

541. 'I honestly feel I could make a difference,' says the aspiring politician. Bets are on over how long he keeps the second word on his tongue.

542. On earth we guard our lives with a selective memory. Away from earth it is not our memory but the complete record of our lives which awaits us.

543. If you experience a dramatic miracle confirming something you have a gut feeling about, over time it will be your gut and not your eye which speaks truth to your mind. The spectacle fades.

544. The world is neither Heaven nor Hell, but it is preparation either for one or for the other.

545. Sometimes in order to obtain a full bottle you first have to empty it. Life's impediments are like the debris, froth and bubbles in the liquid.

546. How many who pray earnestly to their God seek to give to Him as well as solicit from Him?

547. Habits at first are cobwebs, at the end cables.

548. Why does God allow war? You ask amiss; rather enquire why God has seen fit to prevent the wars men *would* have fought had He desisted from intervening.

549. We justify our sins and misdemeanours and make them white in our own eyes. The trouble with driven snow is that it is apt to obscure the path we are supposed to be on.

550. God allows wars only when men protest vehemently against the idea of His interfering in their affairs and disallowing them.

551. When God hides Himself perhaps He's playing a game of hide-and-seek. He knows when you find Him you'll appreciate the discovery.

552. In the midst of the constant, all-pervasive tumult of life there is always a place of peace accessible for the spiritual man to repair to: it is deep inside him.

553. Life is made up of both black and white (certainties) and grey (likelihoods, probabilities and possibilities). Imagine if instead life were solely the chequerboard of the dogmatic, or the uniformly grey sky of the agnostic.

554. War is never fought over scarcity of resources. It is fought over the desire to possess resources by imposing scarcity on others.

555. The colour black is tarred with the brush of evil, the absence of light. But consider its other qualities: one is safety, another mystery.

556. Mother Teresa: 'Do not think that hiding your gifts of God is the sign of humility.'

557. A bird in the hand is worth a thousand in the bush, if the bird is a good man or a good woman. Those are about the odds.

558. The opposite of love is hate. The opposite of love is also indifference. And I for one would rather be hated than rejected or ignored.

559. Are Christians who breathe unending fire and brimstone
     down on unbelievers preaching the justice of God, or the
     punishment they themselves would mete out on unbelievers
     using His name?

560. If you love your beloved in the absence of privation, pain or
     difficulty, then your love is a love in limitation.

561. Look not on the outward appearance. Hearts of stone are
     hidden within the beauty of cherries, peaches and
     tamarinds.

562. Does a worthy master express disappointment in his
     student's failure to achieve, or in his student's failure to
     apply himself?

563. Atheism cannot possibly or conceivably exist. If God doesn't
     exist, self-contradictions exist even less.

564. *Opportunity:* the freedom of a person to exploit his fellow
     man; the freedom of a spiritual person to deny himself that
     facility.

565. Do not presume that a man who utters words of wisdom is
     necessarily the possessor of a soul which has attained to
     their level.

566. Seek not the changeless in a world of change.

567. Does a teacher bestow on his apprentice everything he
     knows? Does he shower indiscriminately on others what his
     wisdom has accrued to him through much labour and at
     great cost?

568. Bellicose men quickly become bored if they run out of
     enemies to fight.

569. Drown your appetites lest you drown in your appetites.

570. It can be incautious to encourage people to pray to God for
     a miracle. How many souls plead to Him to be soothed as
     babies or entertained by the dramatic?

571. For every individual adept at imparting a deep truth in one sentence, there are many who are adept at uttering a thousand sentences of vanity.

572. He spent his whole life living it up, taking all, giving nothing, getting away with it, and dying in contentment. That's good; his soul has it all to pay back – and more.

573. Advice for the distressed: pray to God. Often better advice: listen to God.

574. The arrogant man who considers he possesses all truth often meets deeper truths before his gaze on the path of his life, and he does not see them.

575. Procrastination is even worse than indecision. With procrastination you are not even stirring the rocking horse you are astride.

576. 'He said "God"!' exclaim the religious American public during election time, and install him in office by a landslide. Later they might find out what god he was making reference to, and what use he was making of him.

577. If music be the food of love, then arguments are the indigestion tablets.

578. Politicians like to leave legacies. They like to leg it out of the mess they have created.

579. An insincere man has the ability to smile and frown at the same time from the one face: his lips benign and his eyes malign.

580. A wise son listens to his father; a wiser son listens and watches.

581. He who seeks in his Bible a god who despatches ants with a big hammer will find him. A different God is also to be found therein.

582. You can't see the design of the sampler of your life God is embroidering, and you feel your life's a mess? That's because you're looking at it from underneath.

583. What do religious sects aim to promote? The love of God, or the love of dogma and creed?

584. One rotten apple in a tub, and all of them appear to smell bad.

585. So someone has come up from behind you as you speed through life and he has overtaken you. How do you know you're running in the same race?

586. The best religion is the one which, the more the love of God grows in your heart, the more your religion shrinks to nothing.

587. The sinner praises God with joy for absolving him of his guilt. But does that absolution put back the legs of the man he broke, or the money he emptied from his victim's wallet?

588. To his wife, a good husband and father is a hero. You can say that one who is never at home is a there-o.

589. You will attain the goal of what you believe when your faith in and desire for it exceed your arrogance that what you already believe must be the whole truth.

590. To many Christians, being a child of God means never leaving the nursery.

591. A credulous man hears what a speaker wants him to hear; an aware man sees what the speaker wants him to hear.

592. Jesus was crucified when the Jews demanded of the Gentiles His head. If Jesus returned again as a human being, you can be sure it is the Gentiles who would demand of the Jews His head.

593. I would much rather look into the wrinkled face of an old wizened woman for compassion, counsel, discernment, guidance, patience, understanding and wisdom, than seek these treasures in the flawless face of a tender young maiden.

594. Attend a Christian Bible study and bring up a topic such as out-of-body experiences or UFOs, and your evening will get off to a flying stop.

595. The closest picture of a man who loves a little child properly is that of someone who, with the utmost care, holds in his hands a delicate butterfly.

596. To know something you must experience it. Knowledge alone is not knowledge.

597. Agnosticism, atheism, Buddhism, Catholicism, existentialism, fundamentalism, Hinduism, Judaism, materialism, Protestantism, satanism... One day, 'isms' will become 'wasms'. Islam also: will it become Waslam?

598. 'I believe in God,' you say. So does the devil. And the devil believes in God more than you do: he has so much respect he trembles.

599. 'I don't believe in elephants but I know for a fact tree trunks exist,' says the ant, crawling up an elephant's leg.

600. The spendthrift housewife makes a solemn promise when she borrows extra money from her husband: 'I will pay you back when I get your housekeeping.'

601. Most reincarnationists will get together at a 'Come as you Were' party only if God isn't the one hosting it.

602. To a frightened child, even a direction arrow is seeking a victim to pierce.

603. The reason intelligent life in the universe seems reluctant to show itself on earth among humans is that it is intelligent.

604. Easily the most tragic thing that could ever happen in the life of a glutton is that he should run out of food.

605. Doing what comes naturally makes for fulfilled biology; doing what comes spiritually makes for fulfilled love.

606. You need a spaceship to go into space, but many Christians won't entertain anything more than a bicycle to ride upon the earth; vehicles in space would be waylaid by demons.

607. The secret of loving someone you wait for is to hold your love patiently in your heart, as you would store her ring in a box carefully tied with ribbon.

608. Seen in perspective, a problem is like an ink blot on a sheet of paper: somehow it seems to shrink when your eyes are further back and you notice the other blots around it.

609. A feminist wedding declaration: 'I now pronounce you woman and husband.'

610. Better a has-been than a never was.

611. Six o'clock on the TV: 'Good news, everyone!... There isn't any.'

612. One beholds an evil and dissolute man squandering his life's opportunities. Will he go to Hell? it is enquired. Yes – and beyond.

613. A typical Christian is offered an abacus to help him calculate. 'Too intellectual,' he says, 'I can't understand computers.'

614. Seeking to prove the sufficiency of what you already believe in your present state of knowledge is pouring tar under your feet on the path of your life.

615. A dishonest person has a mouth problem: he suffers from truth decay.

616. Children like to sound rattles and play with marbles. And a room full of politicians has more rattle than a whole can of marbles.

617. What many a prosperity evangelist hears Jesus saying: 'Freely you have received, freely sell.'

618. Suffering is a slough of despond, a trough of blackness. However, if you suffer for God or for your beloved, your ordeal is never bereft of the stark beauty of gems which sparkle from a place of darkness deep within your soul.

619. The lines on an old person's face harbour more stories than those on his palms.

620. Balance is an essential goal in spiritual life, the hewing to the middle of one's path. But to achieve it often entails going to the extremities of the edges of that same path.

621. Before the light of truth, what you have will save you and what you lack will kill you.

622. Science seeks to demystify and religion to mystify. Wisdom seeks to discover.

623. People born into fortune have silver spoons in their mouths. They who work hard to build their lives speak more eloquently, because it is their hands which are full and not their mouths.

624. A baby is the picture of innocence. Tyrants and murderers were once babies. God is not interested in looking at pictures; He likes to study X-rays.

625. 'Of course you can't have been Napoleon in your past life,' asserts the ordinary and insignificant man, 'because I was.'

626. Don't rely on a capricious child. Can you predict when and where and how often a restless fly buzzing in a room will land?

627. I'm a one-woman man. I'm very wise. One at a time.

628. Those who do not live do not love, and those who do not love do not live.

629. Fear cannot understand love, and love cannot understand fear.

630. If a bride at her wedding is a particularly jealous person, she will hear the words 'forsaking all others' and wonder who all these others are.

631. It's no use trying to talk to someone who won't listen: sound doesn't travel through a vacuum.

632. A party animal is so named because somebody coined an accurate metaphor.

633. Do you expect the calmness of a reflective mind to be resident in a flighty teenage girl? Does not a jelly wobble at the slightest touch of the plate?

634. A narrow mind is often behind a wide mouth.

635. To be an atheist demands you be irrational. For if you can reason over it, then there is a God.

636. Be as good a person as your dog takes you for.

637. Two qualities that ought to share the same bed but often don't: intelligence and common sense.

638. One good thing about nightmares is that they often end with the dawn.

639. Faithful words are often not pleasant, pleasant words often not faithful; the well informed do not dispute, they who dispute are not knowledgeable; he who is wise is not always learned, and he who is learned is not always wise.

640. Just because they're not on your road doesn't mean they're lost.

641. Your love for a soul who is dead towards you cannot be rejected, because a soul that is dead cannot receive or return it.

642. Don't entrust the guarding of your food to a dog.

643. Growing old is mandatory; growing up is optional.

644. The devil flatters that he may deceive, charms that he may injure and allures that he may slay. How do you rate the judgment of his worshippers?

645. The Love of God is indeed infinite. But it is manifested, not in forgiving the infinitely unrepentant, but in infinite mercy towards the repentant.

646. Be prepared, when you age, to have the answers to many things which very few people will care to ask you about.

647. Better to think well of a person and be proved wrong than to think ill of a person and be proved wrong.

648. Better to think ill of a person and be proved wrong if you have reason to consider you may be misled.

649. In this world half of the people are the kind who take advantage of the other half.

650. Once the speed cop was a nobody; now he's a man with a badge and a uniform.

651. Sometimes, the value of a thing is understood only when you forsake it, if it has not already taken flight.

652. Put a personality behind the face of a plain person and it is not hard to fall in love with that person.

653. In life a chain can be stronger than its weakest link; all it needs is for the other links to bear some of its load.

654. You have met a nice girl; to foul things up, ignore this sequence: friendship before love, love before respect, respect before commitment, commitment before fidelity, fidelity before sexual relations.

655. God speaks to His children in their hearts; physical signs lack the depth for what He wants to say to them.

656. First impressions count, because people like to think they're right first time and that they're excellent judges of character.

657. Are people who are overly proud of their offspring's achievements trying to make up for the deficiencies in their own characters?

658. Don't let your past dictate who you are, but make it a part of who you aim to be.

659. The man might be head of the family, but who is the neck that turns the head?

660. A cottage is a hovel to a king and a castle to a pauper.

661. On the path of life, one's goal is not the finishing line but the path.

662. Faith is seeing a miracle and not being in the least surprised.

663. The most important thing for a writer isn't publication but the expression of his mind and heart. Second is the exercise of what talent he possesses. Fame and profit should not be ranked among these two.

664. So you would rule the world? To verify the wisdom of your ambition, journey into space and then look back. The little round ball you can just make out, the isolated island swallowed up in infinite blackness, is that same confined habitation you would be master of.

665. Those who do not seek truth avoid doing so because they know they will discover something they cannot turn away from.

666. People believe in evolution, not because it's true but because it's a way of deluding oneself there is no God.

667. Would you be the hero and save the world? First ascertain if you possess enough strength to resist being sucked down by it.

668. Money doesn't bring happiness, but it sure is a means of exemption from unhappiness.

669. The death of love comes to pass, not when love turns to hatred, but when it empties itself of all interest in the beloved.

670. *Paranoia:* just because you *think* it's going to happen doesn't mean it's not.

671. Fifteen minutes of fame to display your lack of talent, and fifteen years for the reputation it has gained for you to dissipate.

672. The more you desire proof, the less you desire truth.

673. Long is the night when you are sleepless, long a mile when you are tired. And long the journey of a soul who hides his face from the Law of God.

674. Those who desire to be spiritual seek the book to be opened to them, but the goal of the quest for enlightenment is to open the book yourself.

675. True growth comes from basking in solitude with oneself.

676. The world: 'She dares to wear scanty or provocative attire in public.' God: 'She dares to display what ought to be concealed.'

677. If a person tries to give you his power do not hasten to accept it, for why is he thus disposed? Is it out of fear, credulity or lack of self-responsibility?

678. Someone asks you who God is. Does he want the truth? If he does, he already knows deep inside him.

679. Don't expect to be validated by your life in the world; validate yourself by addressing yourself to the tasks you are here to perform.

680. People disbelieve in God in the same way they refuse to acknowledge their neighbours, friends or family.

681. If people are going round in circles, where are they coming from and where are they going to?

682. Do we try to impose truth on others, or do we help them find it for themselves?

683. Often, people who direct their anger at you are actually looking in a mirror.

684. For every American evangelist who preaches that God gives a person the power to become spiritual, there is another who preaches that God gives him the power to get wealth.

685. Zombies may be good film entertainment, but they show a deep truth: that a dead soul may reside in a body very much alive.

686. *Vanity:* a talentless and attention-hungry person who thinks he is a somebody. *Great vanity:* a nobody who thinks he is a somebody because of his connections.

687. People are like ships steered through a choppy sea. Their cargo is made up of heavy round balls, rolling to one side or the other. If you encounter a balanced person you have found a rare thing: a master of himself.

688. God makes a man a king, not to give him occasion to be proud, but to challenge him to be humble.

689. A hare-brained man: one who arranges to have his body frozen in the hope of waking up in the future. Who wants to return to driving a clapped-out old banger on earth instead of flying effortlessly among the stars?

690. You are a criminal who has died and escaped the due recompense for your life. Which would you like first – the bad news or the worse?

691. You are guarded over a man who attacks others with too much vigour. Be likewise with the man who defends himself from accusation with too much vigour.

692. Would you be truly great? If a poor person is humble before you, seek every means of lifting him up and abasing yourself.

693. Better to be chastised more sorely by your God than less sorely by a worldly judge.

694. If you do not take another's power, he cannot give it to you. And do you really want to be a vampire?

695. The ability to explore spiritual realms by direct experience does not of itself render one a spiritual person.

696. If we decide we are going to find happiness in the future, then the future is where happiness will remain.

697. You who eschew belief in things unseen because you might be deceived by the unknown, take care you are not deceived by your scepticism.

698. Healthy growth in Christian broadcasting and organisation: growth in spirit or expansion in commercial clout and slickness?

699. Which is the greater company boss? He who sits regally behind his desk in his opulent office or he who takes up a broom among those who labour for him?

700. Two shopkeepers: one put a little too much in the weighing tray and took some out again; the other put in so much and added a little. The wise will know instantly which of the two gathered around him the more customers.

701. The spiritual man watching a crime thriller on TV is embarrassed by the capacity of men to inflict woe on their fellows. The evil man watches to see how to become a more effective criminal.

702. Which is better? To hate the person, or hate what he does which is offensive to you?

703. A person who demands respect doesn't deserve it; he who commands it does.

704. If a fat American were suddenly to find himself in Heaven his first impulse would likely be to look for the burger bar.

705. Which is the uglier? The ravishingly beautiful maiden with lips frozen in conceit, or a woman of marred and distorted features who manages a smile? Wrong question; only one of these is ugly.

706. The greater civilisation? The settlers in America whose children squander non-renewable resources like there's no tomorrow; or the native peoples they looked down on who managed the earth's resources with regard to tomorrow?

707. A balloon blown up is at once bigger and emptier. As is a famous person famous for being famous.

708. The poor man wonders where he is going to get his next loaf of bread from; the rich man where he is going to get his next Rolex from.

709. A rich man finds himself at a loss what to do with his vast wealth. Has his journey in life erased from his mind the needs of the world – or has he himself hidden his heart from them?

710. When the student is ready, the master will appear. When the master is ready the student had better appear.

711. Be wise towards Love: it has more than one opposite. Hate, yes; but are there not also fear, jealousy, indifference, self-regard…?

712. 'That person's going to be mine,' resolves the admirer. A heart set to possess – and perhaps dominate.

713. On the outside looking in? Yet the air where you are stood might be much fresher, and you will see the stars if you look up.

714. Success is often like a dog that keeps chasing a car and suddenly catches it.

715. It is a grievous thing for felons to go unpunished and foreign criminals in a land to escape expulsion. A cancer unchecked is an invitation for it to spread.

716. It's not what you know but whom you know: a shame in the affairs of men, but a true advantage to him who knows his God.

717. To study loneliness, contrast the solitary man surrounded by the silent walls of his room with the famous person surrounded by his garrulous hangers-on. And there is more relish to the cocktail in the hand of the former.

718. Life is a game that is no game.

719. Be careful when asking questions about things you may not be ready for the answers to.

720. Be careful to respect him who has authority over you. You know not who has appointed him to his task: God or man.

721. A cut flower in a vase: fair to behold and soon to die.

722. As Æsop's dog, upon beholding his reflection, lost both the bone in his jaw and its insubstantial counterpart, so will the thief, upon perceiving his true self, loose his grip on his illicit gains.

723. A dead fish fits well into this world: it rots from the head.

724. Rather than feel sorry for someone, exercise compassion: you can feel the former yet be devoid of the latter.

725. How much spiritual worth is infused in the works of a writer who puts pen to paper for money and fame?

726. The seeker enquires why the worshippers are so full of the noise of praise towards their God. 'Because our religion works for us.' He then enquires of a man in quiet solitude why his countenance displays deep serenity and joy. 'Because my religion works for others.'

727. A soldier respects the general in authority over him. Do you credit such a one for discharging his expected duty? But when a general respects the soldier under *him*…

728. The gambler is supremely happy with his winnings, the bank robber with his loot, the lecher with his conquests. But where in their hearts is true joy?

729. Lust is not good. But neither is lust evil. It is the perceptions and intent propelling this force which are the arbiter of whether lust is either the one or the other.

730. If a self-important man is the Earth, his ego is the Moon. When he turns his ego in the direction of the Sun of Truth there is an eclipse.

731. Will evil ultimately conquer good, or will good ultimately conquer evil? The answer lies in discerning which of these states harbours within itself the seeds of its own destruction.

732. The world considers that the accomplishment of one's goal demands ceaseless action. The spirit discerns how accomplishment is attained by desisting from ceaseless action.

733. True beauty is possessed by the woman who can elicit true admiration without fixing her face, hair or clothes.

734. Can a man pursue the prizes of fame, power and wealth, and his spirit be untainted by self-regard?

735. There is a way to tell if a person has exhausted all the chances his true friend has given him. And that is to see if the cup his true friend has given him is fully dry at the bottom.

736. Why does that woman settle for such an indigent man? Easy: she tossed a coin and complied with the outcome: either heads (untrustworthy rich man) or tails (reliable poor man).

737. People address themselves to the challenge of climbing the mountain simply because it's there. And they duck and weave past the challenge of climbing the hill to behold their God simply because at the top He's there.

738. Love means worrying whether your beloved is betraying your trust. Deep love means worrying whether you are betraying your beloved's trust.

739. A lump of clay is destined to become a crystal. All it needs is for its constituent parts, which it shares in common with a crystal, to be reorganised from chaos into order.

740. A wise man to his fellows is sharp but not cutting, pointed but not piercing, straightforward but not unrestrained, brilliant but not blinding.

741. Two men, one rich and the other poor, next to each other and dying in a hospital. One wails, 'It is the end!' The other cries, 'It is the beginning!'

742. The man who takes full credit for what he has achieved in his life is like a brush in the hand of an artist taking credit for a painting.

743. Who is the hero? He who is born with strength and resources and who multiplies his life? Or he who is born in weakness and who overcomes adversity and attains to a life?

744. Light flooding into a place of darkness obliges those who dwell therein to see their shadows.

745. Don't expect the utterance of a person of chaotic thought to be followed by, or to follow on from, an utterance in harmony with it.

746. Better a broken crystal than an intact brick.

747. If you walk a path of suffering and your path is spiritual, then flowers cannot help but sprout up from between the cracks.

748. A child has a right above adults to promises made to him –
or to a thorough explanation for a promise unfulfilled. His
prior right arises from the deeper level of trust he lays
before his guardian.

749. The only objection to the Bible is a bad life; a good life
provides insight into the bad dealings within its pages.

750. Many cats are the sure death of a mouse.

751. Bad odours arise from the disorganised elements of good
odours.

752. A man overly vociferous in his condemnation of another is
likely to be guilty of qualifying for the same sins.

753. The way to escape the shadows in the valley is to escape
the valley.

754. The amount of love you feel in life is equal to the amount
of love you give out in life.

755. Religion has power: if you don't control it when you put
your hands to it, it will control you.

756. A smile: the most beautiful gift you can give someone. Oh,
sorry: it has to be genuine. Uh? No, of course not, you
don't suddenly switch it off. Yes, of course, your eyes need
to be facing in the same direction as your mouth.

757. If you find yourself attached to someone, take care you are
not detached from yourself.

758. If you are rejected by those whom you have not rejected,
then they have rejected themselves.

759. A book: *The Fortunes of Murder Victims*. You are
paralysed by the page depicting their mangled lifeless bodies,
the blood, the gore. Turn the page: their spirits have soared
in joy to meet their angels.

760. A king who has begun to find wisdom: 'I am tired of
ruling over slaves.'

761.   A son learns how to live from a good father. If opportunity presents itself, the last thing he will learn from him is how to die.

762.   Can Satan seriously expect to retain a family of followers, when, if he teaches them well, they cannot escape destroying each other?

763.   If people are building blocks, then loving people erect a beautiful palace, materialistic people a nondescript dwelling and evil people a grotesque pit. And each block is shaped to fit only where it belongs.

764.   It is an ordeal for an evil man to meet his Maker. Can it also be an ordeal for his Maker to encounter him?

765.   He who basks in his religion is someone who admires a door instead of stepping through it to admire the garden.

766.   Death is a law and not a punishment. But unfinished purposes and tasks may render it so.

767.   Are you in love with a person who does not return your love? Or are you in love with *unrequited* love – love of the idea of love?

768.   Where to escape the afflictions of the world around you? In a desolate place? In a dark hideaway? In a secret chamber? Go within.

769.   He who lives beyond his means will die beyond his means.

770.   A master is often imperious to his servant when he does not allow himself the time to be polite.

771.   Those who are zealous for their different religions are like the nuts of a walnut cake recipe that refuse to emerge from their shells in the mixing bowl.

772.   What we know is paltry. What we do not know is immense.

773. Why do you mourn over what you have never lost? Over what was never meant to be?

774. Someone who worships his beloved and puts her on a pedestal is apt to have his illusion shattered when she steps down from it.

775. 'Sorry, it was out of character for me to do that – I was drunk.' It wasn't out of character to blame something else.

776. Don't be deceived by a person's tender exterior; a thin layer of opaque softness obscuring a thick layer of unyielding hardness.

777. Religious differences in tolerance and respect draw men together; religious differences in arrogance and hostility set men apart.

778. Let the past go: what you have grown from is not who you are growing into.

779. Better to realise truth in life than awaken to it after death.

780. The mastery of a master is understood by those of his followers who exercise mastery over themselves.

781. He who is wise keeps his wisdom close to himself, while he who thinks he is wise flaunts his knowledge to all and sundry.

782. To build something higher may call for the tearing down of something lower.

783. Lesson for do-gooders who decline to visit recompense upon criminals and instead try to understand them: the moment you violate the life of another you rescind the right to your own.

784. It is not a bad or messy death which destroys a soul but a bad life.

785. There are many ways to measure success. To a business tycoon, a wise man with few possessions and low status is not a success.

786. Christian rock is exactly that: a rock in a field of music containing large stones of sparkling crystal and other precious gems.

787. By the constant fall of water drops is a pitcher filled.

788. You cannot win over hearts to higher principles by employing the devices of lower principles.

789. The value of a gift is the degree to which you gave of yourself.

790. Those who do not punish the bad are in reality aspiring to the injury of the good, albeit unintentionally.

791. The lecher who has conquered the body of a woman has suffered a grave defeat.

792. To reject light entails embracing darkness; neutrality is not an option.

793. Actions speak louder than words – but actions have stiff competition if the words erupt from a preacher whose sermon concerns money.

794. Evil cannot be undone by resorting to the remedies evil itself would employ.

795. Mindset: you want a better car. You get a better car. Mindset: you…

796. Set up a target and you can be sure it won't be long before someone appears as if by magic and tries to shoot it down.

797. A worldly judge pronounces judgment before opening the door of mercy; a spiritual judge opens the door of mercy before pronouncing judgment.

798. A king appears to be master of all he surveys. Who surveys the king's heart?

799. People seek knowledge from within sound, noise and bustle; the wise man seeks knowledge in silence, serenity and stillness.

800. Better to die standing for life than to live standing for what dies.

801. Two wise men, one wiser than the other: 'Why are you the wiser?' 'I had the better teachers.' 'And what were those?' 'The mistakes I made.'

802. Is true gratitude expressed by imposing a gift or by offering it?

803. Desisting from bad actions does not make one a saint. Bad actions are underlain by bad intentions.

804. Lust in love demands the control and directing of your passion; lust in base desire demands the relinquishing of control and direction to your passion.

805. It is human to fall but angelic to rise again.

806. Mother Teresa: 'Make loved the love that is not loved.'

807. Is a sexual act virtuous or a vice? By its fruits shalt thou know it.

808. A good servant carries out the wishes of his master with promptitude; an excellent servant carries out the wishes of his master without prompting.

809. Is lust virtuous or sinful? Observe: the same carnal forces are in play within as without the marriage bond, and souls, even saints, are born from that union.

810. You write a best-selling novel or music piece. But what would it profit your soul if you gained the whole world and attracted a bad following?

811. If you tire of service to mankind you are serving religion; if you tire not of serving mankind you are serving love and light.

812. 'If God is love He wouldn't send people to Hell.' *Point missed.* It isn't what God is; it is what evil people are.

813. A society bereft of understanding rehabilitates criminals from their evil; a society governed in wisdom eradicates evil from their criminals.

814. A deep thought. In this world of dark, the law of gravity is downwards; but in the world of light an evil soul can drown by sinking upwards.

815. Better to be solitary than surrounded by sycophants and hangers-on.

816. The whispering of a wise man in this world is thunder in the next.

817. Everything is foreknown, but man is free.

818. Mother Teresa: 'Knowledge will make you strong as death.'

819. Christians aspire to save the whole world for God. A world whose purpose is to serve karmic delusion does not need saving for God.

820. To believers no proof is necessary; to non-believers no proof is possible.

821. If a spiritual work is a best-seller, then either God or the devil is the author of it.

822. It is a struggle to build up a reputation in a fickle world; an even harder struggle to maintain it... and ridiculously easy to lose it.

823. The Christian mindset as summed up by many of its adherents: 'We don't need to exercise the brains in our heads because we are happy exercising the faith in our hearts.'

824. There is evil in the world, so belief is abandoned in God who allows it. Result: there is yet more evil in the world, so belief is...

825.   A man is following a religion alien to yours more faithfully than you are following your own. Pray tell me, what credit will you give him?

826.   Love your enemy. Whom you love, you do not fear.

827.   If you look towards darkness, darkness will look up at you. If you look towards light, light will look upon you.

828.   The vanity of celebrity beauty: there's always another one itching in the wings to replace you on the stage the moment you've exhausted your brief and unstretchable span of years.

829.   A real-life contrast in American preachers: one with an established ministry loud on gaining wealth for souls by the name of Creflo Dollar; one with an itinerant lifestyle loud on gaining souls for God by the name of Arthur Blessitt.

830.   An unavoidable choice: hard work or a hard life.

831.   Silence is good for a wise man; even better for a fool.

832.   Minutes are more important than years: wring profit out of every one of your minutes and your years will abound.

833.   The judge says, 'Here is the evil you must avoid which I must punish. The priest says, 'Here is how to avoid this evil and the judge who would punish it.'

834.   Are people addicted to crime dramas on TV because they're aggrieved at real-life criminals who escape apprehension for their crimes, and who escape punishment even when they are apprehended?

835.   What devils you don't deal with in your life will certainly deal with you.

836.   God is wise: He gives a man two eyes and two ears in his head, but only one mouth.

837.   Are you able to figure out life for yourself? Then you don't need religion. But you still need faith, because you are sure to find out you are not self-sufficient.

838.   True love means always having to say you're sorry.

839.   Is the death of a Christian an instant passport to Heaven? Is turning up for class an instant passport to an educational award?

840.   Advice for Christians who want to preach: use words as a very last resort, with the minimum of volume, and even then with the very greatest reluctance.

841.   Heaven: opportunity to bring advantage to the soul of another. The world: opportunity to take advantage of the soul of another.

842.   In the world of high finance, fortunes are routinely won and lost by gambling on the misfortunes of others. In high Heaven no one gambles.

843.   Satan worshippers think it's cool to go to Hell. Are they reading their thermometers the right way up?

844.   Acknowledging your sins and faults is right to do; flagellating yourself over them is overkill.

845.   Three secrets of spiritual life: liberty without licence; nourishment without gluttony; pleasure without debauchery.

846.   Self-control is better than self-denial.

847.   The way to rise above the seven deadly sins is to transform each of them into seven living virtues.

848.   Name-droppers and the attention-hungry associates of the famous are kin to common parasites: both absorb unearned nourishment from sources above the deserving of their own virtue.

849.   Love and mercy seek to rescue a soul from his vices by transforming them into virtues; cold justice destroys vices and often the owner of them.

850.   In Heaven, people admire you for who you are; in the world, people admire you for how you look and what you have.

851. Love warns before executing judgment. Lovelessness executes judgment and asks questions later.

852. A righteous man has regard for the life of his beast. But not so righteous if at the same time he harbours disregard for his fellow man.

853. Home sweet home; house loveless house.

854. Three things which are fickle: the endurance of fame, the security of money and the love of a shallow woman.

855. The thirst of love is to have thirst quenched; the thirst of true love is to thirst and be thirsted for.

856. All butterflies were once caterpillars.

857. Take care what you say to your children: they will repeat word for word what you were rash enough to utter.

858. If you have to beg someone's love, what value has the love so procured?

859. Satan worshippers are not strong on the small print of his terms and conditions. His introductory offers are not gifts but short-term loans; they attract astronomical rates of interest and swingeing penalties for default.

860. There is no greater gift than to know your life has benefitted another.

861. The knife which butters your bread also cuts your throat.

862. A person who is an atheist by denying belief in a God who allows evil does himself no favours: he denies the means to discover why evil is thus allowed.

863. Addictions are like inflation. The value of your money goes down. So you print more notes. So the value of your money goes down. So you...

864. The soul who is afraid of dying fully can never learn how to live fully.

865. You're stuck on a railway crossing and about to be run over by a train. Choose one of the following urgent prayers (arranged in alphabetical order) to save you instantly: Allah! Brahma! Buddha! Jesus! Krishna! Muhammad! Rama! Vishnu!

866. Which is the lower life form: the king of beasts which kills out of hunger, or the king with his retinue who kills for sport?

867. The meaning of life is life: no life, no meaning.

868. If you minimise the truth about darkness you maximise its potential to work its work.

869. God asks you to sacrifice for the greater good of the world; the devil insists on your sacrifice for the greater good of himself.

870. Self-gratification does not serve the soul; it serves the self.

871. The test of love before and within the act of sex is how you behave towards your partner after the act of sex.

872. Love is not an emotion but a decision and an action: love is the cake, and loving emotions the icing atop it.

873. Do not allow the fallibility of a sacred writing to deter you from imbibing the sacred truths within it. Truth may be a difficult business, but is a gold nugget diminished by the mud clinging to it?

874. He who demands of God why He doesn't prevent evil in the world is likely to be of the opposite persuasion regarding the evil in his own life.

875. Wisdom instructs without the noise of words, without the confusion of opinions, without the clash of arguments.

876. Sufferings from God upon your life are to be embraced as remedies, not punishments. Some vices are dealt with only through the application of pain.

877. The light within a man of darkness saves him when his darkness drops away from him. And the darkness in a man of light saves him when it also drops away from him.

878. A true religious sect is not one which seeks to be right, but one which seeks to be true.

879. The music of water: a gurgling brook, the rushing of a waterfall, the lapping of waves upon the shore, a shower of rain cascading through trees, raindrops from a leaf falling into a pool on the ground or against a windowpane in the wind, the trickle of a stream over stones, the stillness of a silent pond.

880. Alexander the Great was conqueror in all his battles, but victories are the fruit of both a wealth of counsellors, and having an army behind.

881. Self-sacrifice is madness to the unspiritual; sanity to the spiritual.

882. A car driver stopped by a traffic policeman has power to overwhelm that officer, but only a fool would proceed to drive on over him. Yet how often do we habitually drive over the guardians of our consciences?

883. Protection is from above. Therefore to earn protection in your life, protect those below you.

884. True mercy is not kindness towards your enemy, but kindness towards your enemy when you are in a position to crush him.

885. When religious sects bicker and argue over who is right, the truth gets lost or forgotten in the quarrel.

886. Humility is a great sin to a sinner, and a great virtue to the virtuous.

887. Ignorance may be bliss – but it ain't freedom.

888. A hero undeserving of his honours is a god to his worshippers but an upstart to those in the light.

889. Extend kindness to Jehovah's Witnesses or Mormons. To smite with cold truth is earth-shattering for souls whose foundation is wafer-thin or shallow.

890. Love at first sight? Can you truly love one whom you know not?

891. Instead of praying for peace, why not walk in it?

892. People who insist in arrogance that they are right know inside that they are not.

893. Do you wish to purge yourself of your sins because of the pain they have inflicted on you, or because of the pain you have inflicted on others?

894. True freedom comes about only within the bonds of moral certitude.

895. People are two-faced; a true friend speaks well of you behind your back.

896. Be disturbed when week after week you open your mouth in the name of God and your congregation does nothing but whoop for joy.

897. Satan gives you wealth to spend on yourself with no thought for others; God gives you wealth to spend on others and also yourself.

898. When true religions get together they downgrade their differences and upgrade what they share in common.

899. Worry less about the result than how hard you tried.

900. If innocence can be claimed only by a child, then never let me grow up.

901. True freedom is liberation from restrictions, those which are inside you.

902. Happiness will never enter into you from the outside until you recognise that the handle to the door of your heart is on the inside.

903. To receive, let go.

904. To avoid pain and frustration, don't demand the moon.

905. Disappointment is your bedfellow in life. You can either turn to embrace it and aggravate your pain, or roll over with your back to it and dream again.

906. A person can provoke you to anger but he cannot force you to anger.

907. You consider free will as the opportunity to indulge your desires. It is also the opportunity to deny yourself what you want for something better.

908. Your mission in life changes as you change: your mission at this moment in time is to do what you are presently capable of.

909. Expecting without giving breeds discontentment; giving without expecting engenders contentment.

910. You can hear yourself speak falsely and thereby deceive yourself. But can your inner self be so easily taken in?

911. Love in the open heart of a child is like the fire in the open hearth of a warm room.

912. Pray for what you want rather than what you need, and God will give you what you need rather than what you want.

913. When you're at rock bottom you can only go up – but you first need to look up.

914. People who have trouble forming close bonds with others are those who cannot easily live with themselves.

915. An obsession is like someone whose eyes are riveted on a grain of salt on a table, and the whole table appears to him as a salt mine.

916. You desire a big thing? Start with a small thing. Dreams of the future are rooted in what use you make of today.

917. If you clutch onto the bad, God cannot fill your hands with the good.

918. There might be legal loopholes enabling you to do what you want, or enabling you to escape the just recompense for your sins, but there are never moral loopholes.

919. God asks for your worship to enhance your appreciation of Him for your benefit. The devil demands your worship to enhance himself at your expense.

920. Don't compare yourself with others below or above you. Compare yourself with who you were in the past and who you should be in the future.

921. You can change your hair, your clothes, your cosmetics, and even resort to cosmetic surgery, but you cannot change the expression of your soul behind your face.

922. 'By their fruits shalt thou know them.' Behold the fruit of parents: their offspring.

923. Nothing important happens by coincidence. Everything important in life is calculated to lead you upwards to the light – or downwards to the dark.

924. The world gives one guarantee: that no one will get out alive.

925. What is best for us to know is often not the most pleasant thing to hear.

926. Choose which of these actions is of little worth: he who gives an expensive gift out of obligation or he who gives a small gift out of love.

927. Being lukewarm is like wearing one shoe: are you covering or uncovering your feet? And are you inclined to take a walk?

928. If to see her is to love her truly, then to love her is to see her as she is.

929. You can certainly cure your negativity: the only power it has over you is your belief in the power it has over you.

930. It is not the mark of intelligence to be able to prove a thing. It is to be able to see that what is true is true, and what is false is false.

931. You don't love your fellow human being because he is good but because he is your fellow human being.

932. Anne Frank: 'I don't think of all the misery but of the beauty that still remains.'

933. Sympathy is your pain in my mind; empathy is your pain in my heart.

934. True love is seeing your beloved every day, and every day is the first time.

935. Glory is not for those who never fail but for those who succeed by rising up every time they fail.

936. Listen, or your tongue will make you deaf.

937. You can't have everything in life: where would you put it?

938. True love should enter your life unobtrusively and quietly. If it approaches like an ostentatious parade, beware.

939. Envy is seeing your neighbour with a top-of-the-range Rolls-Royce car, and you look contemptuously at your Mercedes.

940. Things which are beautiful, rare and rich in the world are not seen or touched on the outside; they are felt inside.

941. In a mind which is listening, a wise utterance whispered with fewest words and in the quietest tone produces the greatest echo.

942. The consummation of love between two people consists not in gazing into each other's eyes, but in both gazing from joint eyes into the eyes of others.

943. Do you always pray for an answer to your prayer, and never pray to be an answer to someone else's prayer?

944. The poor long to be rich; the rich for Heaven; and the heavenly for love in poverty.

945. Cosmetics serve to increase external beauty; love, gentleness and humility serve to increase internal beauty. Thereby a man may attain to beauty equal to that of a woman.

946. Those who love deeply in life die with a worn-out body enclosing a fresh and vibrant heart.

947. Be wise and do not hasten to return a full answer to someone's enquiry. Is a true answer sought? Or is his mouth animated by idle curiosity, an intent to argue with you or a device to trip you up?

948. Erotic activity is like drinking salt water: drink and your thirst increases.

949. If you want to extend joy to others, be compassionate; if you want to extend joy to yourself, be compassionate.

950. Joy shared is joy doubled. Sorrow shared is sorrow halved.

951. If you want to know what strawberries and cherries taste like, ask a child.

952. A family is a peculiar species of octopus whose tentacles you confess deep down you don't want to escape from.

953. Things may give us happiness, but joy can never visit us from outside.

954. If we don't help each other in life, who will? Aliens from space?

955. Joy is the mist of a sweet-smelling scent: spray it towards others and you inhale the aroma yourself.

956. Enter school to learn an art or a science and you will emerge at the completion of your studies. Enter school to learn knowledge or wisdom and you will never emerge.

957. Are you a person who is truly loved for who and what you are? Or are you a person who is truly loved in spite of who and what you are?

958. Heaven is more a felicitous state of being than it is a place.

959. Success is often a matter of hanging on after the others have let go.

960. Be kind to everyone; many people you encounter are fighting hard battles, though you perceive not their enemies nor their means of defence.

961. If flowers can sprout up from the cracks of a dry riverbed, then love can soften the hardest heart.

962. When she broke your heart what she actually broke was your dream. There are plenty more dreams in the sea. Seek one worth fishing for.

963. You don't lose the battle until you stop trying to win it.

964. Storms cause oak trees merely to put down deeper roots.

965. Life without love is a tree bereft of blossom or apples.

966. If there is anything worth while aiming for, don't look for short cuts.

967. 'You can't take it with you when you die.' Yes you can, lots of it; but it's not your car or your house or your clothes or your money or your wine cellar or your golf club membership or your food larder or your yacht or your...

968. The hardest and most evil soul deserves nothing good because he has not earned anything good. But still he has a right to love.

969. The greatest miracle is not to fly in the air without falling or to stand on water without sinking, but to walk on the earth and end your life standing on your feet with dignity.

970. To Native Americans, white man speak with loose tongue. The quieter, fewer and less unrestrained your words, the more your ear is open to hearken to words from the wise.

971. Offer a king a penny and he will despise you. Offer a poor person a penny and he will appreciate you.

972. People walk in and out of your life: your true friend also leaves footprints.

973. A king with perpetual intrigue and strife in his palace is poorer than a pauper with love and peace in his hovel.

974. It is a vain exercise to apply cosmetics in order to lend an appearance of beauty not already present. Her eyes and mouth belie it.

975. Solitude is being alone and being un-lonely.

976. Rich man: so much money, so little time;
Poor man: so much time, so little money.

977. How many people are there in the world? Five billion? Then there are five billion religions in the world. Each one incorporates a god to be worshipped and who demands life's rhythms be conditioned by obedience to him.

978. Most people tell it like it is. Fewer people tell it like it can be.

979. The accomplishment of a great and noble task is founded on the accomplishment of everyday, ignoble tasks being accepted as noble.

980. Look at the world from a mature and experienced mind, but always through the eyes of a child.

981. Regard a battered old car and you may rightfully desire a new, sleek model. Regard a battered old person and you may treasure that person for ever.

982. Is the number thirteen unlucky? How about Jesus and the Apostles? Like many other things, the devil appropriates numerals as his own.

983. A people being in the majority regarding a thing – whether that thing be scanty attire on women or modern music – is not a sufficient arbiter as to the rightness or goodness of it.

984. Dressing expensively is not the same as dressing smartly. A humble plain frock neatly pressed sets off her beauty more than a grotesque ill-fitting outfit from a fashion house.

985. To drain yourself of energy, argue with someone over his religious beliefs. The faithful cling to their persuasions as a limpet to a rock and a drowning man to a lifebelt.

986. People laugh when you tell them recompense will eventually be required of their misdeeds. They've got a sense of humour. They're going to need it.

987. Never allow praises over your life to escape from your own lips.

988. The strongest, the most durable and the most all-embracing thing there is in life is love. It has to be: it covers a multitude of sins.

989. Why do you try to take by force what you could acquire by love?

990. Better marriage be entered into with great difficulty and escaped from with haste than be entered into with haste and escaped from with great difficulty.

991. He sees farthest who flies highest.

992. *Sioux American Indian:* 'As a child I understood how to give; I have forgotten this grace since I became civilised.'

993. The absence of war is by no means sufficient for the presence of peace.

994. A man's life consisteth not in the abundance of his possessions. The paucity of his wealth may well be the saving of it.

995. Seek not strength to be greater than your brother, but seek strength to be greater than yourself.

996. The siren song of cohabitees: 'Not being married means we can opt to choose each other every day.' Yes, and being God in your own life, at much more liberty to abandon that sacred unit.

997. You cannot promote or initiate yourself to a higher level. Promotion and initiation are states nobler than your own, therefore conferred from a level higher than your own.

998. If placed among inferiors you are tempted to strut and to swagger. But can you posture thus when thrown among your equals?

999. Are religious words necessary when one's deeds are holy?

1000. However potent the miracle, as a burning match is impotent to rekindle the fires of a burned-out ember, the light of faith cannot penetrate the faithless.

A Chinese method of torture: death from a thousand cuts.
A gift from spirit: life from a thousand drops of rain

1001. An unbeliever worships one thing above all else: his unbelief.

1002. Three ways to find yourself deeply trapped: waking up after dreaming of flying; awaking to find yourself in a loveless marriage; and finding yourself in a broken elevator in company with a zealous evangelist.

1003. Man is neither as free as he feels nor as bound as he fears.

1004. The Christians have their Bible, the Muslims their Koran, the Hindus their Vedas... and social workers have their training manuals.

1005. A religious man brings religion to other people; a godly man brings God.

1006. If thou be an unbeliever, thou hast a justifiable fear of pain: the torment of pain is a conversation between thee and God.

1007. A son without a father or mother is like a house without a roof or heating.

1008. Rather than pursue knowledge, pursue what use to make of it once you have acquired it.

1009. The effect of small changes:
Women write: *Woman: without her, man is nothing.*
Men write: *Woman, without her man, is nothing.*

1010. He who denies to him who has offended him opportunity to redeem his debt will only increase offence to his own soul.

1011. Ever wonder what goes through criminals' minds when they watch crime thrillers on TV and the rogues are consistently bad shots, they are discredited by everyone else, and they consistently get their comeuppance? So do I.

1012. Fast track to the perdition of a people: reward failure and exempt the guilty.

1013. A test of which side of the Tree of Life you are on: replace the missing comma in: 'Condemn never show mercy'.

1014. The world is a circle, full of tycoons, lechers and idlers. One has so much money, so few women; one has so many women, so little time; and one has so much time, so little money.

1015. Preach the Love of God to the lost; or show the Love of God to the lost?

1016. It is more important to know your enemy's tactics than it is to know his name, his appearance or his taste in brandy.

1017. If you fall in love with the wrong person it is harder to swim than if you fell in a vat of thick treacle, and that fully clad.

1018. Love is like an aeroplane: fall out of love and you will be hurt.

1019. A man does not die when his breath ceases; a man dies when his heart ceases... though he continue thereafter to live in endless pleasures year upon year.

1020. Make new friends, but keep the old; those are silver, these are gold.

1021. People who live solely for the present clap even louder when it comes as a surprise or gift-wrapped in ribbon.

1022. He who always insists he knows the answer to your question is less convincing than he who does know but who is ready to concede ignorance against another question.

1023. It is difficult to recognise your own value when you overly compare yourself to the value you see in others.

1024. Let us be thankful for our lot, even if it isn't.

1025. If thou be an unbeliever, thou hast even less wisdom than a disbeliever. The latter at least owns a reason for his state of being.

1026. Which to choose in the religious marketplace: Buddhism, Christianity, Hinduism, Islam, paganism...? Dost thou seek the breast milk of affection, warmth and love; or the meat of the wisdom and knowledge of spirit?

1027. Would you raise a good child worthy of you? Then you must also raise yourself worthy of him.

1028. Are you sure because it's true or because you are being dogmatic?

1029. In studying human behaviour, it is less important to ask 'What?' 'Where?' 'How?' 'When?' 'How big?' 'How far?' 'How many?', than it is to ask 'Why?'.

1030. Which evangelical preacher or religious operation am I to support? Should it be A? Or is it to be B? Or perhaps it is C? Or maybe it ought to be D? Or could it be E? Or even F?... Not so terrible a decision. By their bank balances shalt thou know them.

1031. Embracing the fad of paganism among a truly spiritual Christian people is trading a jet plane for a horse and buggy.

1032. Hesitate before rejecting something because it is old-fashioned. Ask yourself why it is it has managed to last into the present day.

1033. Is Buddhism superior to Christianity, Hinduism, and Islam? Is Christianity superior to Buddhism, Hinduism, and Islam? Is Hinduism superior to Buddhism, Christianity, and Islam? Or is Islam superior to Buddhism, Christianity, and Hinduism? Be thou not ignorant: look closely at the history and condition, not of an individual devotee, but of a people.

1034. The fool says he no longer believes in Santa Claus because the tooth fairy told him.

1035. Execute a miracle with dazzle and fanfare and people will pay attention to the dazzle and not the miracle.

1036. A woman attracts a man by her charms in the same way that a sausage attracts the hungry by its sizzle.

1037. If pleasure seekers were admitted into Heaven, their first thought would be to wonder when the nightlife would start.

1038. The worst form of injustice in the whole world lies in the heart of an unjust judge who declines the power to dispense justice.

1039. A philosopher is often a man who devises elaborate mental schemes to dress the illogicalities and failures of his own kind in the garb of reason and success.

1040. Proof that commercial Christianity is alive and well: 'For your love offering of $20, we will give you this *free* book on God's way to manage your finances.'

1041. Are you serving someone if you go out of your way to answer a question, the solution to which he can find himself?

1042. Can the inner beauty of a woman shine through an over-application of cosmetics?

1043. The siren song of religious sects: 'Don't rely on yourself; we are the only ones who can make you happy.'

1044. A hard wall which, upon your colliding with it, returns to you pain, also echoes back to you truth.

1045. Anastasia: 'You cannot creep your way to the truth.'

1046. Launder filthy clothes and they become white; launder money and it becomes filthy lucre.

1047. Give a person a feather bed and he will luxuriate on it; offer him grapes and he will open his mouth in expectation.

1048. To the world you may be just one person, but to one person you can be the world.

1049. A man who casts a spell in order to inflict woe on someone is like a man who throws a boomerang with a grenade of evil attached to it.

1050. He who solely lives for the present is condemned to live in the past, for the present waits for no man, and the past is exactly where the present recedes into.

1051. Don't fix what ain't broke: genetically modified crops, chemical additives, bodybuilding steroids, growth hormones, inorganic fertilisers…

1052. God put me on earth to fulfil my purpose. Right now I'm so far behind I will never die.

1053. A man accustomed to solitude may well taste the bitter cup of loneliness once he rejoins the company of his fellows.

1054. Whispered words of love are sweet nothings; silently enacted deeds of love are sweet somethings.

1055. Can he conquer who vanquishes his outward adversaries but remains prey to the adversaries within his own soul?

1056. Do not hasten to open your mouth until you have first ascertained that your hearers are disposed to receive your words.

1057. Infinity: all that is visible must go beyond itself.

1058. The message of many evangelists: God is a canvas on which you can paint your requests. How many recommend instead that you should be a canvas on which God may paint His blessings?

1059. Study the pebbles on a beach or gravel path: you will find some stand out as quite interesting and pretty. But extract the best of these and place them in a container of precious stones.

1060. God writes straight with crooked lines.

1061. A woman with good clothes is an eye-catcher; a woman with a good heart is a dreamcatcher.

1062. When a man is to die he prepares to give up the ghost. As for me, when I die I will prepare to give up the body.

1063. Fire spreads more quickly if its fuel is tinder-dry, and fruit is never sweeter than to the starved.

1064. Impossible advice to love your enemies? Do you not wish your enemies to love *you?*

1065. Impose your store of knowledge on others and your store remains at its present height; attune your ear to the knowledge of others and your own store grows higher.

1066. Friendship provides a long bridge to span over a long distance.

1067. Wealth and power in the hands of a man deficient in self-control are a bomb with a highly inflammable fuse wire.

1068. Knowledge is proud of what it knows; wisdom is humble over what it knows.

1069. If you have an unanswered question, love what you imagine is behind the locked door.

1070. Treat people at a level higher than they display themselves and they may well raise themselves towards that level. And vice versa.

1071. If you decide you will never achieve your goal, you will achieve that goal.

1072. The man says to himself, 'Why am I still waiting for God to bless me?' God says to Himself, 'Why am I still waiting for that man to talk to me, seeing that he wants me to bless him?'

1073. It's not what you're going through that matters, it's what you're going to.

1074. Happiness is not doing what you like but liking what you do.

1075. Do not fear moving forward slowly; fear only not moving at all.

1076. St Thérèse of Lisieux: 'One cannot attain the end without adopting the means.' And so a ladder has rungs.

1077. Don't rush interminably through your life; stop and inhale the scent of the flowers.

1078. If you find you have only one breath left in your body, reserve it for the words 'Thank you'.

1079. If a rich man's life is filled to the brim with his fortune and wealth, who can give him what he needs?

1080. To disregard the elderly is to neglect this morning where you are going to sleep tonight.

1081. The way to loosen and unravel a tightly knotted piece of rope is to let go of your grudges and forgive people.

1082. You cannot help birds of worry flying over your head, but you can see to it they don't build nests in your hair.

1083. It is my birthday: my neighbour has given me flowers; my friend has given me a new hammer. He knew what I wanted.

1084. A rubber band is effective only when it is stretched. Adversity is good for your soul.

1085. Misfortune is good for your soul: all your false friends drop away from you.

1086. Read or listen, not to embrace, nor to contradict, but to weigh.

1087. Sometimes, a cult is what people with closed or narrow minds call a religion they don't like.

1088. A novel is a coherent flow of events leading to an artificial conclusion. Real life is an incoherent succession of events leading to a natural conclusion.

1089. When a wise man dies, it is a library being emptied of its books.

1090. If you have never found reason to call upon God because you've never had a crisis in your life, God will send a crisis into your life.

1091. Tribulation in your life doesn't mean there is no God; tribulation in your life means you are a member of the human race.

1092. Many people are vegetarians for health reasons. I avoid meat because I don't savour the idea of eating what used to have a face and nursed its young.

1093. A brightly coloured glossy envelope drops through my letter box, together with one that is bland and plain. I throw the one away, but am drawn to the other: it bears a handwritten message from my friend.

1094. A brightly coloured glossy envelope drops through my letter box, with a long coded serial number adjacent to the words 'Dear Sir...' I throw...

1095. I lean toward the company of a child rather than toward that of an adult. With a child I can let myself go, wear old comfortable clothes, even neglect to shave. I can dare to be me.

1096. Love at first sight. If it is your soulmate it will also be love at last sight. And there will never be a last sight.

1097. Don't rush in to help a child until you know he's done what he can to help himself.

1098. If the devil threatens you, have more fear of following him than defying him.

1099. If you try your utmost and fail, you will have peace because you did what you could.

1100. Women need regular transfusions – are they of diamond rings and necklaces; or of hugs, kisses, sweet words and flowers?

1101. I am an only child and so is my brother. Yes, I came into this world alone, I will leave it alone, and every man is my brother.

1102. Be a first-rate version of yourself, not a second-rate version of someone else.

1103. You're never too old to grow up.

1104. Perfection is not expected of you by your true friend; it would astonish him if he got it from you.

1105. Responding to kindness with ingratitude is repelling rose petals with a high-pressure hose.

1106. Non-slothful parents who orbit around their child make *him* slothful.

1107. Everyone is in awe of a lion tamer in a cage with his beasts. But there is an exception: those who teach in schools.

1108. Look at a sausage: you don't imagine it as the product of a pig. And a man is equally proficient at concealing his sins.

1109. Study the most recent works of science, but the most ancient works of wisdom.

1110. Devils and despots say a thing they know isn't true. They figure that if they keep saying it it will be true.

1111. Viewed in the world, you are born at sunrise, live through the day and die at sunset. Viewed from above the world, you are born at sunset, live through the night and die at sunrise.

1112. The crucible: at ten, impulse is sublimated; at twenty, emotion; at thirty, will; at forty, mind; at fifty, judgment; at sixty, virtue; at seventy, spirit; at eighty, wisdom; at ninety, understanding; at one hundred, submission. Hearken to the old who have submitted.

1113. Life is fragile: handle with prayer.

1114. Do you wish for blind obedience from your servant? Or do you wish to open his eyes as to why he must obey you?

1115. The Bible and other holy books impart all knowledge and wisdom which can be known; men know the rest.

1116. Youths pride themselves in being total rebels. And when they get together they copy each other slavishly.

1117. To his dog a man is a god, and it has eyes for no other. Thereby is the root of the popularity of dog ownership.

1118. Finesse, gentility and breeding: the art of concealing how much we think of ourselves and how little we think of others.

1119. A friend will side with you when you are wrong; nearly everyone will side with you when you are right.

1120. A common religious mentality: attend English classes for a month and you are Shakespeare's equal.

1121. Childhood shows the morning as manhood shows the day.

1122. Learn what will stretch you. An oversize coat is one you can grow to fill; an undersize coat will constrict you.

1123. Oh, for romance! I refuse to get my coat wet in the rain, to have gnats bite me in the swamp or to suffer indigestion with an overfull stomach.

1124. The art of dying: I've read the book; now I'm going to see the film.

1125. The Old and New Testaments are a Bible in words. A wide-eyed child delighted by flowers in a meadow, or a soldier giving succour to a wounded adversary, these are a Bible in pictures.

1126. The prince married the princess and lived happily ever after: a good story. The prince married a pauper and made her a princess: a beautiful story.

1127. In a decadent society, children are educated more by their peers than they are taught by their teachers.

1128. Is it better to waste your life, or to do nothing with it at all? Answers on a postcard, please.

1129. Fall in love swiftly; grow in love slowly.

1130. Shout, and everyone hears you; speak, and those around you hear you; be silent, and your friend hears you.

1131. A practising doctor is understood to be proficient in his field, true to his calling. Is a practising Christian one who is proficient in *his* field? Or one practising to be true to his calling?

1132. Do couples love each other bountifully out of selfless love – or to the minimum out of the fear of losing their conjugal advantages?

1133. If she wears just enough for modesty, then she is immodest.

1134. In sex education, children learn how to mingle bodies. Are children given to learn how to mingle hearts and souls?

1135. There is one thing worse than being talked about, and that is not being talked about.

1136. Did someone say wars are started by homo sapiens?

1137. You've worked hard: you want to live in a first-class-quality home, to drive a top quality car, to wear excellent quality clothes, and to consume rare quality food. And have you worked to become a high quality person?

1138. There are no apples more delicious to a child than apples which are scrumped from an owner's garden behind his wall.

1139. Success is a dicey business. How long will you give it before you detect the stirrings of envy and resentment in your friends and acquaintances?

1140. Heaven and Hell. Is there a place for the agnostic? Is there a fence dividing these two abodes for him to sit on?

1141. A man who rushes through life and allows no time to inhale the scent of the flowers enjoys rushing more than he enjoys flowers.

1142. The Lord giveth and the Lord taketh away. The devil loaneth and the devil snatcheth back.

1143. If you seek to know what lies ahead on the path, ask someone who has already travelled down it.

1144. Do not be ashamed to be declined by a woman. A woman's prerogative is to be pursued by many suitors, and she cannot accept them all; a man's prerogative is to decline to pursue for equally desirable alternatives.

1145. Time does not heal wounds; a change in attitude heals wounds.

1146. Popularity is people liking you; happiness is you liking you.

1147. The ever-widening gap between the poor and the rich in a society: there are the have-nots and there are the have-yachts.

1148. If you desire to be loved, first love.

1149. Who said praying had to involve matters of great import? A woman of faith can share with God that her cake failed to rise in the oven.

1150. Liars, insincere politicians and rogue religious leaders are together accomplished alchemists: they possess the ability to transmute hot air into a cold solid.

1151. A true soldier goes to war because he is prepared to be a hero; a conscript goes to war because he is not prepared to be a hero.

1152. Good people don't need laws to govern them. Bad people not only need laws, they seek to defy them at every turn. At least a mindless machine which breaks down simply waits to be repaired.

1153. Celebrity costs a beautiful woman dear: how long do her countenance and her face hold out against the ravages of fame and adulation?

1154. An immeritorious or base work that is a best-seller is like an infectious disease. It sells well because it is selling well.

1155. Definition of a child: a soul whose tears can be transformed into instant smiles with the slightest waft of a wand.

1156. A Bible teacher quotes scriptures to 100% accuracy, solicitous not to alter any jot or tittle. Is that teacher displaying understanding of spirit, or demonstrating his prowess for exercising an unerring eye for linguistic detail?

1157. Religion: more a recipe for division and hatred than for unity and love. Proper faith? The reverse effect.

1158. Every man is like every other man, is like some other men, and is like no other man.

1159. You may consider yourself eloquent, a crafter of fine words; but silence is sometimes the best answer.

1160. If a parent desires to teach his child the way he should go, he should first have travelled that way himself.

1161. The best relationship to have with someone is one in which your need for each other is exceeded by your love for each other.

1162. You are a spirit in a material body: you can be happier with who you are rather than with what you see in a mirror.

1163. A good-time girl aiming to prolong her dissolute ways: let me eat, drink and be merry; for tomorrow I diet.

1164. The Secrets of Even Greater Sex, no. 38244: great sex has you screaming God's name during the act; even greater sex has you whispering your beloved's name after the act.

1165. The Secrets of Even Greater Sex, no. 38245: in great sex you think about the body of your lover; in even greater sex the soul of your beloved.

1166. The Secrets of Even Greater Sex, no. 38246: in great sex emotion is expressed through the generation of friction; in even greater sex emotion is expressed through the healing over of friction.

1167. The Secrets of Even Greater Sex, no. 38247: great sex has you waving goodbye at the end of an encounter; even greater sex has you saying hello as you step over a sacred threshold.

1168. An excellent virtue: do to others what you would have them do to you. Be yet cautious: others have different principles and values.

1169. 'A proverb is one man's wit and all men's wisdom' – so said a philosopher. A living proverb is the wit and wisdom of God channelled through one man and made to make all men wise.

1170. As measuring devices possess varying degrees of sensitivity, so one person may suffer more than another when the same misfortune befalls them both.

1171. A miracle of God: magic until you're shown how it's done?

1172. If you have to be forced to apologise and to forgive, then you have begun neither to apologise nor to forgive.

1173. You may lack wings to fly, but if you have true freedom you can soar to heights no bird can dream of reaching.

1174. Does the strength of an edifice lie in its towers leaning on each other, or in their standing upright side by side? If you and your beloved are of a spirit to be borne by each other, then you are not ready for each other.

1175. He who gives and harbours remembrance of his deed has given less fully than he who erases in his heart all trace of remembrance.

1176. If the hand does not move the stick, the stick will not move anything else.

1177. A man may hope to live for ever; a religious man looks forward to living for ever with God; a wise man prepares to live for ever with God and with himself.

1178. When you want something you've never had, maybe you need to do something you've never done.

1179. Which is the greater? The waters of a vast ocean – or the tears you shed?

1180. Every man possesses two characters extra to that of his true self: that which he thinks he has, and that which he shows to the world.

1181. Is he who is the most accustomed to teach the most reluctant to learn?

1182. The bigger mistake is not apologising for it.

1183. With God you don't sail a boat with no storms to weather; you sail a boat which will not sink, whatever the weather.

1184. An ass laden with books is an ass, not a scholar.

1185. Is the book you are reading the expression of its author's own thoughts, or is it the thoughts he intends will be those of his readers?

1186. The less inclined you are to keep a secret, the more curious you are to hear it.

1187. Talking about a pot of rice does not cook it. And the key to success is of no use until it is inserted in the lock.

1188. The best throw of a dice is not a six but away.

1189. If you would pray to God, don't expect the builder to erect your house with a flick of his finger. A house is built brick by brick, and you can watch him do it.

1190. To make a discourse more interesting, minimise it.

1191. There is nothing worse than being a slave to doubt and suspicion. Slavery to doubt separates: it is a poison which disintegrates friendship and pleasant relations. And suspicion is a barb which hurts, a sword which kills.

1192. A timid person is afraid before danger, a coward during danger, and a courageous person after danger.

1193. Technology devoid of prudence or wisdom, and a servant becomes a tyrant, and then an executioner.

1194. Education turns a fool into an educated fool. And sex education turns lust into knowledgeable lust.

1195. Without woman, where would man be? In a decadent modern society, down the pub or at a football match.

1196. It is the nature of a great mind to be calm and undisturbed.

1197. The opposite of a religious fanatic is not an atheist but a person who couldn't care less, if only because an atheist is a religious fanatic.

1198. To be remembered after we have gone is poor recompense for being treated with contempt while we are here. And how many epitaphs reflect the true hearts of their authors?

1199. If you bite your superior, it is the wound of your superior which will mend.

1200. Before sex education: boys and girls are children in role play as mummies and daddies. After sex education: boys and girls are mini-grown-ups in real play as mummies and daddies.

1201. What cat doesn't eat fish?

1202. The poor don't need the lesson of economising. The rich don't need to learn how to be extravagant.

1203. In company, never posture as the more learned. You may be expert in your discipline; others will be more expert than you in theirs. Tell someone the time from your watch only when asked; and a Rolex may well speak of vanity.

1204. Failure isn't falling down; it's staying down.

1205. If someone gives you a drop of water in kindness, think of how you may repay him with a flowing spring.

1206. To understand a woman doesn't mean you can understand any other woman.

1207. The love of money is a root of all evil. The lack of money can be another such root.

1208. An earnest writer writes, not because he wants to but because he has to. The prospect of a readership is a secondary consideration.

1209. Would God, who endowed man with sense, reason and intellect, intend that in the pursuit of faith we forgo their exercise?

1210. Fashion is the science of how to seem rather than to be.

1211. If war is an adventure, it is only ever the adventure of a disease and the periodic bursting forth of a suppurating sore.

1212. If what you read evokes no worthwhile thought in your mind, perhaps its themes made no such demand on the mind of the writer.

1213. What is beautiful may pass away; what is lovely will always pass into new loveliness.

1214. When a man tells you he became rich through hard work, ask him, 'Whose?'

1215. We are not human beings on a spiritual journey; we are spirit beings on a human journey.

1216. Marriage is like a cage with open bars. Birds see food inside and want to get in; others see freedom outside and want to get out, and this is the freedom they failed to appreciate before they got in.

1217. Confining your reading to words can be an unprofitable exercise. Better read the direct experience of life.

1218. He who regards the five senses of materiality as the sum total of reality is the same as someone who thinks the horizon is the boundary of the world.

1219. 'First they ignore you, then they laugh at you, then they fight you, then you win.' (Gandhi)

1220. Don't be so humble; you're not that great.

1221. A true master seeks no disciples. If he would make a true disciple, he will cause that person to hang, not onto his words, but onto the truths above and beyond both of them.

1222. Be as careful of what you read as of the company you keep. Your habits and character will be influenced as deeply by the former as by the latter.

1223. Beware the fury of a patient man as you should beware of God's.

1224. If a traveller visits a country better than his own, he may discover the inadequacies of his own. But if he visits a country worse than his own, he may learn to appreciate his own.

1225. Most people talk so they won't have to listen.

1226. Care when others don't; forgive when others can't; understand when others won't.

1227. Make a living by what you get; make a life by what you give.

1228. We are pencils: what we do leaves a mark, what we do can be corrected, what we do comes from inside us, what we do periodically requires sharpening, and what we do is good only when guided by a wise Hand that holds us.

1229. If you think you can, you might; if you think you can't, you won't.

1230. The Bible might never praise intellect; neither does it over-esteem the vanity of those who possess it.

1231. Reading is to your mind what physical exercise is to your body.

1232. 'A witty saying proves nothing.' (Voltaire) A display of wit boosts the ego of a person, but sharing wisdom boosts the spirit of a hearer.

1233. True freedom is not bestowed; it is achieved.

1234. Do you see difficulties in every opportunity, or opportunities in every difficulty?

1235. Never refer to him as a mere child. A child will always be preferable to a mere adult.

1236. 'Although the world is full of suffering, it is full also of the overcoming of it.' (Helen Keller)

1237. The definition of kindness depends on whose it is: strength (God's); weakness (the world's).

1238. A girl aged between sixteen and twenty-three thinks of herself as beautiful as a peony. Like all flowers, peonies begin to fade.

1239. When he who is heading for the sun looks back, he can see only his shadow.

1240. He who serves his employer for money rather than love will find it less likely to gain from life either the one or the other.

1241. Outward beauty is like a young woman ascending the throne at sixteen. She expects to reign until she is seventy-five but instead lasts only until she is twenty-nine.

1242. When you work out a problem, don't think about beauty but only how to solve the problem. But when you have finished, if the solution is not beautiful you'll know it is a wrong answer.

1243. No one ever teaches well who wants to teach, nor governs well who wants to govern.

1244. A leisure room without books is like a body without a soul.

1245. The mediocre teacher tells. The good teacher explains. The superior teacher demonstrates. The master inspires.

1246. Common sense is better than intelligence. An intellectual may well devise a way to dig hard ground; common sense may well wait for the ground to soften.

1247. The test of good manners is one's patience over bad manners.

1248. Being poor means your neighbours close by are solicitous to ignore you; being rich means strangers from afar are solicitous to know you.

1249. Today is the tomorrow you worried about yesterday.

1250. Do not hasten to accept an opportunity to be master over others if you haven't first learned how to be master over yourself.

1251. The history of the human race summed up in one sentence: wars have never been won; only intermissions.

1252. When did I realise I was God? Well, I was praying one day and I suddenly realised I was talking to myself.

1253. Atheism is first a disease of the soul before it becomes a disease of the brain.

1254. The strange effect of money on people: if you pursue it you're avaricious; if you keep it you're a capitalist; if you spend it you're extravagant; if you don't amass it you're an idler; if you don't pursue it you've no ambition; if you acquire it without working for it you're a parasite; if you fail to spend it after working for it you are a fool.

1255. An egotist: a man more interested in himself than in me.

1256. Romance is the art of balancing what you want to gain from the other person with the appearance of what you want to give.

1257. A peach was once a bitter almond.

1258. Great men are rarely isolated mountain peaks; they are the summits of mountain ranges.

1259. You don't have to win first place to be a winner.

1260. It feels so good and we're supremely happy (the world); it feels so right and we're supremely happy (Heaven).

1261. If one wise word does not succeed, neither may ten thousand be sufficient.

1262. Facts of life, no. 69829: In a society you don't make the poor richer by making the rich poorer.

1263. A friend's eye is a good mirror.

1264. Employ your spare time profiting from the writings of others, so that you will easily come by what these others have laboured for.

1265. A good teacher imparts not only knowledge, but the desire to go after it.

1266. Lovest thou thy fellow man? This day, to how many ill-minded persons hast thou shown a well-minded disposition?

1267. Great men can make other men feel small. Very great men can make other people feel great.

1268. Offer too much help to a beggar and he will claim your property.

1269. Proud of your woman's love for you? Understand that many a woman loves a man, not because he is a man, but because he is not a woman.

1270. Try before you rust.

1271. The only reason a fool smiles in the midst of danger is that he's too stupid to know that's what he's in.

1272. An eloquent and forceful preacher provokes questions. Ask yourself if you will become like him if you follow what he says.

1273. Beware of two things: a slow enemy, and a sudden friend.

1274. A person is superior to a computer when (a) he does what his master instructs, and (b) he is able to refuse what his master instructs.

1275. When your work speaks for itself, don't interrupt.

1276. A powerful mind requires a more powerful self-discipline. A pond is to be found in a meadow; but a mountain envelops a lake.

1277. Beauty without virtue or love is a flower without scent.

1278. Different actions, same result: explaining your position to an opponent of fixed thought; and flogging a dead horse.

1279. When dogs are many they do not fear wolves.

1280. Those who know how to win are much more numerous than those who know how to make proper use of victories.

1281. Letters, telephone calls, emails? Yes, you can talk to them without having to look them in the eye.

1282. If you will not dare to enter the bear's den you can never capture bear cubs.

1283. Self-regulation with two opposite results: allowing the fox to guard the hen house (in Heaven); allowing the fox to guard the hen house (in the world).

1284. Opportunity is often overlooked because it comes dressed in working clothes.

1285. Don't be concerned with growing old, unless you are thinking about your mind and not your body.

1286. There are glances of hatred that stab, and raise no cry of murder.

1287. There are people who want heavenly joy in their hearts, but they don't want it in Heaven.

1288. The way to Heaven is turn right and straight on.

1289. Reading the work of a writer does not make you a know-it-all, unless what you know all of is the writer's own personal view.

1290. Secular education teaches one how to read and gain knowledge; it does not teach one how to discern the value or worth of it.

1291. Once the wound is healed, forget the pain.

1292. Lonely? If you have love in your heart you are never alone: there is always someone or something you can share it with.

1293. The difference between an idiot and a computer is that a computer is a fast idiot.

1294. There are two kinds of men who never amount to much: those who cannot do as they are told, and those who cannot do anything but what they are told.

1295. Failure isn't pausing to rest when tired, it's falling asleep.

1296. Don't hire a man whose sole concern is to work for money, but rather him who works also for love. Then pay him more than what he asks.

1297. God does not need to work a miracle to convince an atheist. His mundane works are enough.

1298. Don't stay in bed unless, aside from making love in bed, you can make money in bed.

1299. Better never to receive a kindness than never to bestow one. And to fail to return kindness is a sin greater than to fail to confer one.

1300. By far the hardest years of your life are between the ages of ten and your deathbed.

1301. If you want to ascertain God's and the devil's attitudes to money, look at the people they give it to.

1302. I have not failed. I have merely found a hundred ways that don't work.

1303. As one pip can start an apple tree, and one spark can start a conflagration, so can one word reconcile an enemy and one smile start a friendship.

1304. Don't take advice from a man who works only with his mouth.

1305. God brings about endings which are fulfilled. If you are unfulfilled, then you haven't finished with God, nor He with you.

1306. What is everyone's business is no one's business.

1307. A city street with buildings covered in graffiti and ground strewn with cigarette ends, trodden-in chewing gum and food remnants is like a very scruffy house with a disgustingly filthy carpet.

1308. Don't hide your talents. What use is a sundial in the shade?

1309. The average human body is 70% water and 30% everything else. The average human soul is 30% spirit and 70% everything else.

1310. Only light can drive out darkness. And only love can drive out hatred, not hatred.

1311. If you love liberty, you can love others. Love power, you love yourself.

1312. Modern life statements to be placed in order of believability: 'Free of charge!'; 'Totally free of charge!'; and 'Absolutely and totally free of charge!'

1313. Religion is the answer, says the preacher. What question is religion the answer to?

1314. Your carbon footprint is the measure of how forcefully you imprint the shape of your foot by stamping it into the face of the world.

1315. The woods should be poorer if no bird save the perfect genius sang therein.

1316. You may not have a reason to smile, but if you manage one you may well give someone else a reason to smile.

1317. You cannot change the direction of the wind, but you can adjust your sails.

1318. Believe when others doubt; work when others dream; save when others spend. You will succeed when others fail.

1319. What is important is not the years of your life but the life of your years.

1320. When you see a mouse laughing at a cat, there must be a hole somewhere. And youths in a decadent society laugh at those who would discipline them.

1321. Do not look back at where you fell but at where you slipped.

1322. Beware of an overbearing neighbour or one constantly turning up. A friend respects your privacy more than your communion.

1323. The object of any war is not to die for your country but to make sure your enemy dies for his. In any case, on life's battlefields, who is ever willing to sacrifice his life for you?

1324. If you are a success in any people's eyes other than your own, you are not a success.

1325. Men: competition is a sin: destroy your competitors;
God: competition is a sin: cooperate and do not compete.

1326. Distance tests a horse's strength, and time a man's character.

1327. A work is to be received in the same spirit in which it is given. How does a stomach receive its diet of modern entertainment?

1328. Do convictions enslave free minds – or free enslaved minds?

1329. A little knowledge makes a man conceited; much knowledge makes him humble.

1330. The difference between a human being brought in a spaceship to live on another planet and a dog brought to live in a house? None: both are creatures forced to adapt to an alien environment.

1331. You cannot help whom you fall in love with, but you can decide whether and how to express it.

1332. A gambling house promises to be socially responsible. And a robber promises not to shoot the bank tellers.

1333. When a woman opens her legs for money remember that it is her legs that are open, not her heart.

1334. Congratulations, now that you see in your mirror grey hairs, wrinkles and sagging cheekbones: you have perfect vision.

1335. How to confuse your rational thought processes: gaze intently at a beautiful flower in your hand and say to yourself, 'It evolved.'

1336. Precision bombing: murdering one person instead of a thousand and one.

1337. As blood is thicker than water, so is truth thicker than blood. Do not shield your son from the recompense due his wayward deeds.

1338. Be honest, even when others are not; even when others will not; even when others cannot.

1339. The plainness of a woman's face is more than compensated for by the engagement of her personality.

1340. A deaf composer or crippled artist is a beggar who places riches and jewels before kings.

1341. If man lacks God or a religion he invents one. And if a people run out of enemies to fight they look round for new adversaries.

1342. Fast track to loss of freedom: exercise your freedom to be indifferent to what looms up and threatens to dictate your life.

1343. Peace is not the same as the absence of war. Peace is the absence of war in people's souls.

1344. The best judge is one with a stern face and a kind heart.

1345. Fundamentalist Christianity fully expects future rapture of the faithful. What it might experience is future rupture.

1346. Has he who is offended by the strange appearance of an alien being cause for shame if he becomes the recipient of love and respect from that same being?

1347. It is no cause for shame to hide your religion from those who may object to it. It is a great cause of shame if you hide from them the One whom you worship.

1348. Upholding the rights of a criminal by disregarding his responsibilities is brother to destroying the rights of his victims.

1349. In an unsafe world it is good to advise children not to accept sweets from strangers. It is equally good to advise adults not to give sweets to strange children.

1350. Is it that the man is a homosexual, or that you are to desist from hurting someone who is different from you?

1351. What is the strongest bond between you and the one in your family who is closest to you? Is it your blood? Or your spirit?

1352. So you don't negotiate with your enemies. Since you don't negotiate with your friends because they are your friends, what use at all is negotiation?

1353. The true believer – heartwashed or brainwashed?

1354. Three lies uttered by a man: when seducing a woman; when giving a political speech; when having returned from a fishing trip.

1355. Three lies uttered by a woman: when seducing an old man; when applying for a company secretary's job; when putting on weight during a dieting exercise.

1356. What is the difference between a woman who opens her legs for £300 and another who opens her legs for £10? Moral condition or desperation? Or £290?

1357. Nothing unites squabbling people or nations more effectively than a common enemy.

1358. They say one's clothes speak forth the character of their wearer. My clothes say that I care more about feeling relaxed than about the opinions of others.

1359. They say one's clothes speak forth the character of their wearer. But it is not hard to conceal a carcase under a shroud.

1360. Few hear the poor when they shout; the rich are heard when they whisper.

1361. Giving help is like rain in the spring. Begging help is like snow in the summer.

1362. Remorse: 'Sorry.' True remorse: 'Sorry. I'm now putting matters right.'

1363. Competing sportsmen vying for a trophy are like a group of ants around the foot of an elephant arguing who is the biggest.

1364. Satan's favourite Walt Disney film: *Pitch Black and the Seven Goblins*.

1365. Two sources of pain: being robbed by a thief of something precious; and something precious thrust back at you which you sacrificed for someone.

1366. Is knowledge power? Can a car move devoid of an ignition switch?

1367. There's no point in harbouring anguish over things you can't change.

1368. When you are punished for your sin, is it God who is meting out on you His revenge, or is it your body doing it?

1369. The fact that lemmings choose the same path doesn't automatically mean that it's the right path.

1370. In government mindsets, politically correct; in people's consciences, frequently morally incorrect.

1371. A high proportion of people who have sexually transmissible diseases don't know it. A high proportion of people who desist from behaving with sexual abandon know they don't have any.

1372. To judge a man, look at his children.

1373. The best nurse in the whole wide world is he who feels sorry for himself and refuses to pick himself up – a soul who is nurse to his own feelings.

1374. Satan's favourite song: 'I'm dreaming of a black Sabbath.' Gosh, do they have music there?

1375. To judge a man, look at the company he chooses for his friends.

1376. Compassion for the stooped and haggard figure appearing older than her years – her woeful condition the outcome of a lifetime of hardship? Or compassion for that sorrowful wretch when a neighbour whispers in your ear that her harsh years were self-inflicted by dissolute habits?

1377. We don't have leaders in the world today; we have politicians and preachers.

1378. To judge a man, look at the company he rubs shoulders with who are the denizens of the places he frequents for his entertainment.

1379. 'I'm not a product of culture; I do my own thing,' utters the rebellious youth belonging to the fiercest of all cultures.

1380. The contrite sinner cannot look his God in the eye on account of shame; the drug user or drunkard on account of blurred vision.

1381. Self-justification quotation 78173: 'I who am paid handsomely by rich clients for my sexual services will not sink so low as to resort to prostitution.'

1382. Self justification quotation 78174: 'I am a responsible drug user; I will never use hard drugs such as heroin.'

1383. Self-justification quotation 78175: 'I am a banker and, owing to the economic adversity blighting every worker, I am graciously accepting a bonus this year of only £2 million instead of £3 million. I have a social conscience.'

1384. Self-justification quotation 78176: 'I deserve a huge salary increase to put me on a par with other business tycoons. Parity of remuneration is important; justifying what I already get paid is not.'

1385. If there is anything in this life which holds the prospect of surpassing your wildest dreams, then your dreams are anything but wild.

1386. A judge of principles sees black and white; a greater judge sees shades of grey.

1387. Economics A to Z, lesson A: to argue that inflation causes the printing of extra money is to say that wet streets cause rain. Now you know what causes inflation.

1388. The oldest profession is that which is the most profitable: is it prostitution or war?

1389. A quality unexpectedly shared in common between a goldfish in a bowl and an unruly child: a short attention span.

1390. A man who is disallowed from speaking his own mind is a soul in fetters.

1391. You want a special friend: someone to talk to, someone who pays you attention, someone who does his best to understand you, someone who always responds to you, someone who is reliable, someone who is predictable, someone who loves you, and someone who is always pleased to see you. You want a dog.

1392. Does Light defeat the darkness of Evil, or does Evil, an inherent self-contradiction, defeat itself?

1393. 'Jesus is the answer to your need!' the evangelist thumps on his soapbox. The rich and prosperous, if they are listening, wonder who on earth among them can possibly have any need He can be the answer to.

1394. Freedom is not free.

1395. Can the sin of a man with a good heart cling forever to him? Can mud cling to a precious stone washed in a stream?

1396. The deeper problem is not failing to see the solution but failing to see the problem.

1397. The only useful way to compare yourself with others is to define who you are: by distinguishing what you are from what you are not.

1398. Is the proper exercise of faith a focus on how you will live after you die – or on how you live before you die?

1399. A man who feels he is an exile in his own world is inclined to consider himself to be the citizen of another.

1400. The poor: a hand-to-mouth daily existence.
The rich: a Rolex-to-diamond-necklace daily indulgence.

1401. What is the worth of someone who doesn't know, or apply in his life, the difference between good and evil?

1402. Two ways to be fooled: to believe what isn't true, and to refuse to believe what is true.

1403. Are you living or are you surviving?

1404. The true evangelist commends to us the future life as not only conceivable but desirable (after Helen Keller). The prosperity evangelist indeed renders the future life conceivable, but recommends to us the present life as desirable.

1405. To forget one's forebears is to be a brook without a source, or a tree without roots.

1406. A father is zealous to defend his wayward son. Is blood thicker than water, or is it pride which is thicker than self-discipline?

1407. Some people wouldn't recognise the goodness of God if it fell on them. When the sun is out, they need to fold up their umbrellas.

1408. 'Death is not the end of life, but only one of its most important experiences.' (Helen Keller)

1409. To explain the actions of a person in this world, ask the question: 'Who gains?' To explain the actions of a person in a heavenly world, ask the question, 'Who loves?'

1410. War brings people together and motivates them to extraordinary efforts. Just what would they do without it?

1411. All things come to him who waits: be careful over what you decide is worth waiting for.

1412. Poverty in the West is royalty in the Third World. Poverty in the West: a second-hand car, yesterday's mobile phone and failure to afford a foreign holiday.

1413. Satan's favourite adage: many claws make dark work.

1414. In liberal societies, men and women are disposed to give themselves fully to each other on their first or second encounter. Expressions of love – or a low value placed on what they so freely give up?

1415. The first step to winning over your sworn enemy: tell him you want to see things from his point of view.

1416. The booby prize for the way to win over your sworn enemy: 'They're 100% wrong because we disagree with them.' (Lebanese protester, 1 December 2006)

1417. The last soldier to leave Vietnam at the conclusion of the war there was told to turn off the lights. As that war had turned the country into Hell on earth, were there any lights left to turn off?

1418. The problem with global warming isn't excessive atmospheric temperatures but deficient heart temperatures.

1419. 'Although the world is full of suffering it is full also of the overcoming of it.' (Helen Keller)

1420. What a teacher of unruly children dreams of being able to say to his charges: 'Come out of your seat the person who made that pin drop!'

1421. Preachers who tell us we are sinners need not apologise for the message, but they ought to apologise for our embarrassment. The omission of the one may be counterproductive; omission of the other, certainly so.

1422. Young women who like to play hard to get put themselves in the danger of becoming hard to want.

1423. He displays the trappings of wealth: is that because he is wealthy or because his trappings have been gathered by credit – a social climber posturing?

1424. You've had a hard life; perhaps a soft life would have been harder on you by confirming your weakness.

1425. It is said that God does not look upon sin. But since God looks upon both sinners and the self-righteous, what does He see in us?

1426. 'I do not want the peace which passeth understanding, I want the understanding which bringeth peace.' (Helen Keller)

1427. The living know that they will die. But do the evil know that they are already dead?

1428. I would rather know my beloved loves me than that she is faithful to me.

1429. It is only in a dictionary that success comes before work; before effort not even that.

1430. What religion needs is teachers, not preachers. You don't preach knowledge, and believers are kept infants for the want of it.

1431 If principles are important to you, when in Rome do as the Christians did.

1432. To test a person's interest in you, next time he greets you and asks how you are, proceed to tell him.

1433. The greatest love you can receive is from your God, then from his angels, then from your mother, then from your true friend, then from your child, then from your dog, then from your sweetheart.

1434. Is a woman plain on account of her bland features, or on account of a bland, featureless personality? It is by no means beyond her to possess a heart of love, a magic elixir which turns greys into colours.

1435. In the world, your heroes are inaccessible and they are apt to despise you. Prepare to be a nobody in their eyes. In vain you beat yourself to a pulp in your worship of them. In Heaven, your heroes love you and are entirely accessible. To them, you are always a somebody.

1436. A king is habituated to the obeisance of both his subjects and strangers, who bow low in abjection before him. Wherewith, then, shall a king learn humility?

1437. When you have perfect faith, you fear God and no man. When you have perfect religion, you fear both.

1438. If you mount a tiger, don't get off its back.

1439. A friendly demeanour is no indicator of true friendship. Demeanours mould one's face; true friendship, one's heart.

1440. When a stranger bows low before a king who knows him not, and who is known not by him, how can the king know whether it is out of respect or out of obligation that the man bends his neck?

1441. The biggest lie in the whole world is to assert that you've never said one.

1442. Definition of a plastic smile: one which doesn't reach your eyes.

1443. Someone who is a constant critic of a person, never acknowledging any virtue in him, values criticism over a regard for what is true.

1444. You smiled; you said thank you; you looked back; you expressed praise. That's *all* you did? Nay, not all you did; *what* you did.

1445. Artificial sweetener: saccharin. A young lady's recorded phone voice: artificial greeting.

1446. The good know that the good are destined for the Light and the evil for the Dark. The evil persuade themselves that the evil go to the Light out of pure mercy and they could care less where the good go.

1447. Don't take down a fence until you know the reason it was put up.

1448. Many people in the past: 'We wear crosses because we're believers'; many people today: 'We wear crosses because we like jewellery.'

1449. If criminals are not made to be in fear of the law, then we have reason to be in fear of criminals.

1450. So God doesn't exist because you can't see Him. OK: BBC Radio doesn't exist because you're tuned to another station.

1451. Being misled no. 26389: throwing yours hands up in
horror at the atrocity reported in clinical detail in your
newspaper and asking, 'What is the world coming to?'
Maybe, just maybe, the atrocity is newsworthy only
because of the infrequency of its occurrence.

1452. Being misled no. 26390: alas, the murdered girl was
eulogised as the sweetest and most beautiful daughter a
mother could have wished for. Maybe, just maybe, you will
one day read of a murder victim painted in the colours of
an average person.

1453. Being misled no. 26391: receiving a heartfelt letter from a
young secretary apologising profusely for the bad service her
company rendered you. Maybe, just maybe, you will one
day receive such a letter which has not been dictated to her
by someone else.

1454. 'Thank you for your contribution, dear supporter: we love
you,' I am assured by the religious organisation. They love
me, but they do not know me.

1455. Are you the more blessed when God fulfils your desires in
your life, or when God fulfils His desires in your life?

1456. It is dangerous for an unbeliever to take his arguments for a
walk in the country. The country has absolutely no
manners. The sky, the trees, the birds and animals, the
stream and the flowers preach the loudest sermon he will
ever hear.

1457. Empty vessels and American evangelists make the most
noise. When the latter preach about money, they are apt to
get even louder.

1458. Out of all the Mexicans I count as my friends, there is one
above all others who has helped me stay fit and healthy.
His name is Manual Labour.

1459. Have you laboured throughout your life to be rewarded by
      God in Heaven? Or have you lived your life to become
      worthy of acceptance by God in Heaven?

1460. The moving finger writes; and, having writ,
      Moves on: nor all thy piety nor wit
      Shall lure it back to cancel half a line,
      Nor all thy tears wash out a word of it. *The Rubáiyát*

www.ingramcontent.com/pod-product-compliance
Lightning Source LLC
Chambersburg PA
CBHW051454250726
48655CB00001B/414